W9-DEW-380

WITHDRAWN

Are Video Games Harmful?

Hal Marcovitz

INCONTROVERSY

ReferencePoint
Press®

San Diego, CA

For more information, contact:
ReferencePoint Press, Inc.
PO Box 27779
San Diego, CA 92198
www.ReferencePointPress.com

Picture credits:
Cover: iStockphoto.com
Maury Aaseng: 74
AP Images: 7, 16, 21, 23, 28, 40, 48, 61, 69
Landov: 12
Photofest: 33

LIBRARY OF CONGRESS CATALOGING-IN-PUBLICATION DATA

Marcovitz, Hal.
  Are video games harmful? / by Hal Marcovitz.
    p. cm. — (In controversy series)
  Includes bibliographical references and index.
  ISBN-13: 978-1-60152-125-5 (hardback)
  ISBN-10: 1-60152-125-1 (hardback)
  1. Video games and children—United States. 2. Video games and teenagers—United States.
  3. Video gamers—Psychology. 4. Children and violence—United States. 5. Youth and violence—
  United States. I. Title.
    HQ784.V53M37 2011
    794.8083--dc22
                                                              2010006036

Contents

Foreword

I n 2008, as the U.S. economy and economies worldwide were falling into the worst recession since the Great Depression, most Americans had difficulty comprehending the complexity, magnitude, and scope of what was happening. As is often the case with a complex, controversial issue such as this historic global economic recession, looking at the problem as a whole can be overwhelming and often does not lead to understanding. One way to better comprehend such a large issue or event is to break it into smaller parts. The intricacies of global economic recession may be difficult to understand, but one can gain insight by instead beginning with an individual contributing factor such as the real estate market. When examined through a narrower lens, complex issues become clearer and easier to evaluate.

This is the idea behind ReferencePoint Press's *In Controversy* series. The series examines the complex, controversial issues of the day by breaking them into smaller pieces. Rather than looking at the stem cell research debate as a whole, a title would examine an important aspect of the debate such as *Is Stem Cell Research Necessary?* or *Is Embryonic Stem Cell Research Ethical?* By studying the central issues of the debate individually, researchers gain a more solid and focused understanding of the topic as a whole.

Each book in the series provides a clear, insightful discussion of the issues, integrating facts and a variety of contrasting opinions for a solid, balanced perspective. Personal accounts and direct quotes from academic and professional experts, advocacy groups, politicians, and others enhance the narrative. Sidebars add depth to the discussion by expanding on important ideas and events. For quick reference, a list of key facts concludes every chapter. Source notes, an annotated organizations list, bibliography, and index provide student researchers with additional tools for papers and class discussion.

The *In Controversy* series also challenges students to think critically about issues, to improve their problem-solving skills, and to sharpen their ability to form educated opinions. As President Barack Obama stated in a March 2009 speech, success in the twenty-first century will not be measurable merely by students' ability to "fill in a bubble on a test but whether they possess 21st century skills like problem-solving and critical thinking and entrepreneurship and creativity." Those who possess these skills will have a strong foundation for whatever lies ahead.

No one can know for certain what sort of world awaits today's students. What we can assume, however, is that those who are inquisitive about a wide range of issues; open-minded to divergent views; aware of bias and opinion; and able to reason, reflect, and reconsider will be best prepared for the future. As the international development organization Oxfam notes, "Today's young people will grow up to be the citizens of the future: but what that future holds for them is uncertain. We can be quite confident, however, that they will be faced with decisions about a wide range of issues on which people have differing, contradictory views. If they are to develop as global citizens all young people should have the opportunity to engage with these controversial issues."

In Controversy helps today's students better prepare for tomorrow. An understanding of the complex issues that drive our world and the ability to think critically about them are essential components of contributing, competing, and succeeding in the twenty-first century.

When Video Games Are More than Just Games

Police in Wicomico Church, Virginia, were stunned one January morning in 2009 when they responded to the scene of an accident in which a car had run off the road, striking a utility pole. Opening the door of the car, they discovered the vehicle had been driven by a 6-year-old boy. According to the child's story, he had missed the school bus and, fearing he would be late, took his mother's car keys and tried to drive himself to school. Incredibly, the boy managed to drive the car some 10 miles (16km) before the vehicle struck the utility pole. The boy was not injured in the accident. "It's a miracle that somebody didn't get killed," said Northumberland County, Virginia, sheriff Chuck Wilkins. "We're a rural area, but if we do have a rush hour, that's it."[1]

Where did the boy learn to drive? According to the child, he learned at home, playing two video games: *Grand Theft Auto* and *Monster Truck Jam*. Both games are hardly educational and certainly not intended to teach the skills one would need to navigate the public highways safely. Instead, the games are action-packed, intended to provide their players with the thrills of participating in high-speed car chases and smash-em-up action.

Ryan MacDonald, who reviews games for the online video game review site GameSpot, did not find the action in *Grand Theft Auto* suitable for young children. In his review of the game, MacDonald wrote:

Grand Theft Auto is the most violent piece of gaming on the PlayStation yet. Some will find the language and concept of the game to be outrageously humorous, while others will just find it atrocious. If you are a fan of R-rated action movies, then nothing in this game will shock or damage you. However, if you are a parent looking for a game for your 10-year-old, you may want to skip this one.[2]

The authorities did not blame the child for misunderstanding the nature of the games, but they did come down hard on the boy's parents. Both were arrested on charges of felony child endangerment. Evidently, the father had already left for work that morning, and the mother was still sleeping when her son missed the bus and took her keys.

A six-year-old Virginia boy who tried to drive himself to school after missing the bus later told police he learned to drive from video games including Grand Theft Auto, *a game intended for mature players because of violence, language, and content.*

Intended as Entertainment

The incident in Virginia illustrates the degree to which video games have become a part of American culture and how their misuse can become truly dangerous. In this case the boy was extremely lucky. His car left the road and struck the pole after he swerved the vehicle to avoid an oncoming tractor-trailer.

Video games are intended as entertainment—they have been regarded as such since 1961, when Steve Russell, a computer engineering student at the Massachusetts Institute of Technology, figured out a way to get two tiny blips of light to follow his instructions as they drifted across a tiny black-and-white screen. Russell developed the first video game—he called it *Spacewar!* It took a great deal of imagination to look at the screen and envision a battle waged in intergalactic space. The game involved nothing more than the two blips of light firing even smaller blips of light at each other. Nevertheless, today's exciting, challenging, and visually stunning games and graphics can find their roots in *Spacewar!*, a game that took Russell six months to develop, working in his spare time.

It is likely that Russell never envisioned many of the problems video games often present to society. Critics could argue that *Spacewar!* was a violent game—the object of the competition called for the player to destroy enemy spacecraft. Given the simple graphics of the era, players could hardly see themselves actually ending human lives by blasting their opponents out of the sky.

Contrast that experience with the environment in which the gamer finds himself or herself while playing *killer7*, in which an elite band of martial artists battles suicidal terrorists. To survive the numerous violent encounters, *killer7* players can collect the blood of their fallen victims to heal themselves. Meanwhile, to open hidden passages, the players must slit their own wrists, spraying the blood across the scene of the action. Wrote game reviewer Tom Orry in Videogamer, an online gamers' site:

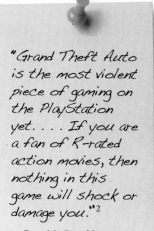

"*Grand Theft Auto* is the most violent piece of gaming on the PlayStation yet. . . . If you are a fan of R-rated action movies, then nothing in this game will shock or damage you."[2]

— Ryan MacDonald, game reviewer for GameSpot.

Combat becomes quite rewarding, with successful one-hit kills bringing a sense of achievement that few games offer. . . . As you move into the second half of the game you genuinely feel like you have the upper hand over the enemy. Then the annoyance factor kicks in again, with one-hit deaths happening far too frequently and a number of cheap in-your-face [enemies] taking you out before you have the chance to draw your weapon.[3]

More than Just Violence

There is much more than just violent content that mental health professionals find troubling about video games. They wonder whether gamers could become addicted to playing the games, spending much of their waking hours glued to their consoles and screens. They wonder whether young people neglect their studies while growing obese on their living room sofas as the only parts of their bodies that seem to get any exercise are the fingers that maneuver the video game controls.

Says David Walsh, a psychologist and president of the National Institute on Media and the Family:

Ten years ago, video games were, by today's standards, primitive and simple. They were gimmicky toys for kids. Today, the video game industry takes in more money than the movie business and nearly everyone, kids and adults alike, has played one of these games. They're not going away, and why should they? They're great entertainment— used in moderation.[4]

Indeed, many critics may even concede that *Grand Theft Auto* can be good entertainment under the right circumstance. That circumstance would be when it is played by an adult or mature young person who clearly understands the purpose and goals of the game—and not by a six-year-old boy who regards it as something akin to a driver education film.

"Ten years ago, video games were, by today's standards, primitive and simple. They were gimmicky toys for kids."[4]

— David Walsh, president of the National Institute on Media and the Family.

Facts

- A Kaiser Family Foundation study found that only 21 percent of American parents have set rules about which video games their children are permitted to play.

- The Pew Internet & American Life Project reports that 21 percent of video game owners play either every day or almost every day.

- The video game *Spacewar!* would help launch an industry that is worth tens of billions of dollars; Steve Russell, who developed the game, never made any money off *Spacewar!*

What Are the Origins of Today's Video Game Controversies?

I n the early 1970s, when the first *Pong* games started showing up in bars, bowling alleys, and pinball arcades, it all seemed pretty harmless. *Pong* was nothing more than a game of virtual table tennis—two players maneuvered electronic paddles, striking an electronic ball back and forth.

And yet, despite what would today be regarded as rather ho-hum action and primitive graphics, *Pong* was enormously successful. The first *Pong* machine was installed in 1972 in a bar named Andy Capp's Tavern in San Jose, California. During that first week of operation, the *Pong* machine took in $300 in quarters while the pinball machine standing nearby did just $30 in business. Even in those earliest days of video game play, evidence of the addictive nature of the entertainment began to surface. Recalled Bill Gattis, the manager of Andy Capp's: "This is the weirdest thing. When I opened the bar [one] morning, there were two or three people at the door waiting to get in. They walked in and played that machine. They didn't buy anything. I've never seen anything like this before."[5]

Ten years after those first players poured their quarters into the *Pong* machine, C. Everett Koop, then the surgeon general of the United States, made a speech in which he warned Americans

Video games got their start with Pong *(pictured), a virtual table tennis game that became an immediate sensation. Though primitive by today's standards,* Pong *developed a devoted following.*

about the dangers of video game play. Koop said he was concerned about the addictive nature of the games as well as their potential for promoting violent conduct among players. "They are into it body and soul," Koop said of video game enthusiasts. "There's nothing constructive in the games. Everything is eliminate, kill, destroy and do it fast."[6]

At the time the graphics of most video games were not terribly advanced from what *Pong* players saw on the screen at Andy Capp's. In fact, the specific game that had raised Koop's concern, prompting him to issue such a dire warning, was *Pac-Man*, a game that essentially required the player to satisfy the insatiable appetite of a little round yellow dot by feeding it other yellow dots.

Why Do People Play Video Games?

Those early *Pong* players certainly did not realize it, but they were among the first fans of what would grow into a huge following.

Today the design and production of video games are part of a $68 billion industry with tens of millions of devoted fans. Indeed, the video game industry makes a bigger profit than the Hollywood film industry.

According to a study performed by the Washington, D.C.–based Pew Internet & American Life Project, more than half of all American adults play video games, with 1 in 5 playing every day. Meanwhile, a poll by the Gallup Organization has found that at least 74 percent of American teens report playing video games at least one hour a week. Gamers range from casual players who may kill a few minutes of downtime by playing virtual solitaire on their office computers to committed gamers who spend hundreds of dollars a year on new games as well as the latest consoles. Many games are played in Internet versions involving online gatherings of thousands of players.

Video games have become part of the fabric of American life. People play them to relax and unwind after hard days at work or school or at home. Sarah Ninesling, a 30-year-old stay-at-home mother from suburban New York, says that after a long day of housework and minding her four young children, she loses herself in such games as *World of Warcraft* and *Fallout 3*, sometimes playing past midnight. Ninesling says she plays to relax, escape, and feel a sense of accomplishment in defeating her virtual enemies. "You are always going to be a hero,"[7] she says of her video game experiences.

Video games can be regarded as simply another development in humankind's long fascination with games. People have been playing games for thousands of years. In the tomb of the Egyptian king Tutankhamen, who lived some 3,300 years ago, archaeologists unearthed a wooden surface split into divisions that appears to have been some sort of board game—it may have been an early version of checkers known as *alquerque* or *quirkat*. An early version of chess was played as far back as the eighth century by the Persians. Card playing dates back to the fourteenth century. The board game Monopoly was introduced in 1935. Moreover, you do not have to be human to

"They are into it body and soul. There's nothing constructive in the games. Everything is eliminate, kill, destroy and do it fast."[6]

— C. Everett Koop, former surgeon general of the United States.

Video Games and Racial Bias

A study by the advocacy group Children Now concluded that a significant amount of racial bias can be found in video games—the heroes of the games are overwhelmingly white, while villains and supporting characters are often Latino, black, or Asian. Even in sports-oriented games, the group found, minorities were often given the roles of villains. "In sports games, African Americans were most likely to display aggressive behaviors," said the organization's report, *Fair Play? Violence, Gender and Race in Video Games*. "Nearly eight out of ten African American competitors (79 percent) engaged in physical and verbal aggression compared to only 57 percent of white competitors. African American competitors were the only racial group to use verbal aggression on the field."

In action-oriented games, the study found that a stunning 86 percent of black female characters were destined to be victims of violence. Said the report, "Their victimization rate was almost twice that of white females (45 percent) and nearly four times that of Asian females (23 percent)."

The Children Now report suggested that young players are likely to draw the wrong conclusions from the depiction of the races in video games. "Any examination of the quality of messages that children receive from video games also requires a close look at how people of color are depicted in these games," said the report. "These depictions have implications not only for youth of color but for white youth as well."

Children Now, *Fair Play? Violence, Race and Gender in Video Games*. December 1, 2001. www.childrennow.org.

enjoy games—any pet owner knows the joy expressed by a dog playing fetch or a kitten chasing a ball of yarn.

Mental health experts have spent years studying why people play games and have arrived at some basic conclusions that should not come as a shock to anyone: They are fun and they fulfill the human desire for competition. They are educational—most young children learn the importance of waiting one's turn by playing games. Moreover, games give people the opportunity to lose themselves in fantasy and role playing, which has been a major part of game playing since long before the invention of video games. Indeed, centuries before the video game *Global Domination* enabled players to develop strategies to defeat enemy armies, chess players were maneuvering knights and rooks across the board to defeat enemy armies.

For video game players, there is an added element—the interactive nature of the games. In board games and card games, the player is often at the mercy of luck. Roll the dice and land on "Go to Jail" in Monopoly and one has no other choice than to go to jail—and hope for a lucky roll of the dice to gain freedom. Draw a pair of jacks in poker, and one's main strategy often rests on the hope that the player across the table does not draw a pair of queens. In video games, though, luck often has very little to do with the course of the game. In most video game play, the participant holds a large measure of power over the game—depending on decisions the player makes, the game's scenario, and the degree of difficulty. Such power, according to Ted Friedman, an author and associate professor of communications at Georgia State University, helps draw the player further into the game, making the gamer a much more active component in the play than he or she would otherwise be in checkers or Monopoly. Says Friedman:

> The player must muddle through the universe of the game—exploring the settings, talking to the characters, acquiring and using objects—until she or he has accomplished everything necessary to trigger the next stage of the plot. In the process, the player is expected to regularly make mistakes, die, and restart the game in a previously saved position.

The idea of computer "role playing" emphasizes the opportunity for the gamer to *identify* with the character on the screen—the fantasy that rather than just *watching* the protagonist one can actually *be* him or her.[8]

The Games Turn Violent

The first video games were not very interactive—essentially, they were simply high-tech (for their time) versions of board games and sports. *Pong* was manufactured by Atari, a company founded by video game pioneers Nolan Bushnell and Ted Dabney. (The term *Atari* means "checkmate" in a Japanese version of chess.) In the beginning, Atari had the business all to itself—eventually, some 19,000 *Pong* machines were manufactured and installed in bars and similar establishments. But other companies soon saw the potential of the video game business and joined the competition. Other early games such as *Space Invaders*, *Gun Fight*, and *Night*

Space Invaders (pictured) and other games of its time took video game playing to a new level, featuring improved action and graphics. Early games such as this were played mainly in arcades.

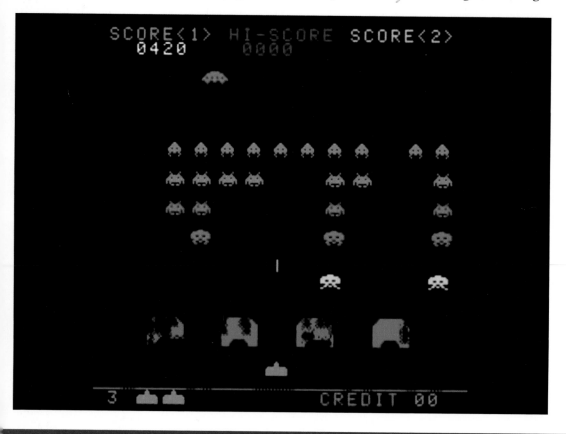

Driver were soon developed, all featuring graphics and action a bit improved over what had been available to players in *Pong*.

In those early years all video games were manufactured in arcade versions—gamers played in commercial establishments, inserting coins in the machines to play the games. But in 1977 Atari released a home version video game console, the Atari 2600, that enabled enthusiasts to enjoy the games on the TV sets in their living rooms. Moreover, the Atari 2600 accepted interchangeable cartridges, meaning players could swap games. Other companies such as Magnavox and Coleco introduced home consoles as well. To illustrate how quickly the industry was growing, in 1982, the year after Coleco introduced its home game console, the ColecoVision, the company announced sales of some $500 million—double the company's total sales of the year before. Most of those sales were attributed to the enormous popularity of *Donkey Kong*, a Japanese-produced game that required a video game character named Mario to jump over barrels rolled downhill by a big ape.

Donkey Kong may have been harmless fun, but the same could not be said of many other games that were finding their way onto the American market. In 1976 the first truly violent video game, *Death Race*, was released in an arcade version. In the game, players scored points by using their cars to run down gremlins escaping from a graveyard. There is no question that *Death Race* was violent, but at least the "victims" of the violence were supernatural characters who more or less resembled stick figures, given the crude graphics of the era. Still, *Death Race* prompted parents' groups and mental health experts to raise alarms. Such national TV programs as *Donahue* and *60 Minutes* produced features on *Death Race* and the growing trend of violence in video games. "It's very tame by today's standards," says Eddie Adlum, publisher of *RePlay* magazine. "Every time you made a hit, a little cross would appear on the monitor signifying a grave. Nice game. Fun. Bottom line, the game really took off when TV stations started to get some complaints from irate parents that this was a terrible example to set for children. The industry got a lot of coast-to-coast coverage during news programs."[9]

"The idea of computer 'role playing' emphasizes the opportunity for the gamer to identify with the character on the screen—the fantasy that rather than just watching the protagonist one can actually be him or her."[8]

— Ted Friedman, associate professor of communications at Georgia State University.

Brutality Grows

As Koop's speech demonstrated, even *Pac-Man* caused some early concerns—after all, the little yellow hero of the game dispensed with his enemies by eating them. But the action in *Death Race* and *Pac-Man* could be considered rather tame when compared with the activities depicted on video game screens starting in the 1980s. Indeed, the fears of parents and others were ramped up a notch in 1983 when a video game producer released three pornographic games, including *Custer's Revenge.* By now the graphics were just slightly improved, but the action had grown much darker. In the game, players maneuvered General Custer as he dodged arrows while crossing the screen. If the general made it all the way across, he rewarded himself by raping an Indian maiden tied to a post.

Again parents protested—and so did civil rights organizations representing women and Native Americans. "Women Against Pornography did a lot of picketing against it," recalled Arnie Katz, former editor of *Electronic Games* magazine. "I remember talking to a representative of that organization and telling her that in my opinion, the best way to keep the game from selling was to ignore it."[10] Instead, the groups kept up the pressure, which drew press interest in the games. When the stories about *Custer's Revenge* and the other games appeared in the media, players wanted to see what they were all about. As a result, Katz says, the national furor over *Custer's Revenge* helped double the game's sales.

Viewpoint of the Shooter

In 1993 the most violent game of the era found its way into the hands of players. In *Mortal Kombat*, players delivered karate chops and kicks to their opponents, dispatching them with death blows that were sure to result in splashes of blood. In *Mortal Kombat* it is possible to slay an opponent through decapitation or by ripping out the enemy's heart. The fact that *Mortal Kombat* was adapted into a movie version spoke volumes about the game's popularity. Said Jeff Greeson, the manager of an Internet site devoted to the game: "*Mortal Kombat* not only stood out, it grabbed you by the shirt collar and demanded your attention. *Mortal Kombat* had the biggest and most realistic characters ever featured in a video game at that time. You were literally watching digitally animated photographs of people flying through the air and beating the living hell out of each other."[11]

A year after *Mortal Kombat* made its debut, another video game ratcheted up the violence on-screen even more. The game, titled *Doom*, enabled the player to hold a virtual gun—giving the gamer the viewpoint of firing the gun from behind the weapon.

Playing *Quake II*: Like the Real Thing

After the release of the so-called first-person shooter games *Doom* and *Quake*, journalist Andrew Phillips wanted to know how lifelike they really were. Phillips had never fired a gun before, so he went to an indoor shooting range in Virginia and fired handguns at a stationary target. Much to his surprise, Phillips found that he had remarkably good aim for a newcomer: 22 of 25 of his shots hit near the center of the target at a range of 25 yards (23m).

"Nothing wrong with that," shooting range manager Ernie Lyles told Phillips after he examined the target. "That's some good shooting. But you know who does the best the first time out? It's the kids. It's all that Nintendo play. It's perfect practice for the real thing." According to Lyles, children as young as 10 are allowed to shoot at the range as long as they are under supervision of their parents.

Next, Phillips obtained a copy of the video game *Quake II*, an updated version of *Quake*. As Lyles suggested, Phillips found the action in the game remarkably similar to shooting a real gun. He also found the game addictive—Phillips played for two hours before he noticed how long he had spent behind the screen. "It demands intense concentration and complete isolation," he said.

Quoted in Andrew Phillips, "The World of Guns and *Doom*," *Maclean's*, May 10, 1999, p. 24.

Doom became the first of the so-called first-person shooter games, giving the player the same viewpoint a real-life shooter would experience as he or she fired the weapon. Not only could the player fire the gun, but enemies hit by the bullets exploded in shockingly graphic detail. And then, in 1996 *Doom*'s designer, id Software, produced *Quake*, an even more graphically violent title. As with *Doom*, *Quake* enabled players to participate in the action from behind the gun.

If anyone questioned the realism of *Doom* and *Quake*, they needed only to check with the American armed services. Shortly after *Doom* hit the store shelves, the U.S. Marine Corps decided to employ video games in its training program for marines assigned to urban warfare missions. Trainers believed that video games could be helpful in honing reflexes for marines who may find themselves unexpectedly confronted by armed enemies. Instead of going through the trouble and expense of developing its own game, the Marine Corps obtained copies of *Doom* and assigned corps members to play the game.

Depictions of Women

According to the scenarios of the games, the enemies in *Doom* and *Quake* are evil villains who deserve to be blown away. That has not been the case in many other video games. In those games women are often featured as victims who are included simply to give the players innocent characters to assault.

The depiction of women in video games has long raised concerns among parents' groups, industry watchdogs, and mental health experts. In 1996 the game *Tomb Raider* was developed by British developer Eidos Interactive. Its heroine is leggy Lara Croft. The shapely character dispatches her enemies with guns strapped to her hips, cowboy style. Teenage boys are her biggest fans, but teenage girls also look at Croft as something of a role model. Girls find Croft empowering. She is the type of heroine who can act on her own, blowing away the bad guys with her own guns. Lara has no need to be protected by a man. Said *Newsweek* magazine, "Lara takes the slogan 'Girl Power' to the next level.

"Lara [Croft] takes the slogan 'Girl Power' to the next level. Call her Shotgun Spice; right in front of you, yet always out of reach, she's the perfect fantasy girl for the digital generation."[12]

— N'Gai Croal and Jane Hughes, writing in *Newsweek* magazine.

Call her Shotgun Spice; right in front of you, yet always out of reach, she's the perfect fantasy girl for the digital generation."[12]

Croft started a trend—women were soon made into featured characters of other video games. Among the female characters who proved to be as brave and as quick with their guns and karate kicks as any male characters are Tifa Lockhart of *Final Fantasy VII*, Chun Li of *Streetfighter II*, Cate Archer of *No One Lives Forever*, and Jill Valentine of the *Resident Evil* series.

As with Lara Croft, these heroines are typically leggy, large-breasted, and often depicted in some state of undress. One study, published by the advocacy group Children Now in 2001, looked at 70 of the most popular video games of the era and concluded that in 21 percent of the games, women were depicted in costumes that revealed at least part of their breasts (in 7 percent, the women

The shapely heroine Lara Croft dispatches her enemies with guns strapped to her hips in the Tomb Raider *game. Other game makers followed this example, developing female characters who were quick, tough, and often depicted in various states of undress.*

were topless); 13 percent bared their buttocks, including 8 percent that were fully exposed, and 20 percent showed bare stomachs. Typically, these female characters were depicted with large bosoms, tiny waists, and long legs. Said the Children Now report, "Females may be as tough as the males, and may have to face similar missions and opponents, but they have an added challenge: to look sexy while doing it."[13] The authors of the report looked at one game, *Command & Conquer: Red Alert*, and found that the main female character, Tanya, "battles the [enemies] in a midriff revealing tank top and leans forward whenever she speaks to expose her cleavage."[14]

An Alarming Trend

Moreover, as video games moved into the 2000s, women were depicted less as scrappy heroines, such as Lara Croft or Jill Valentine, and more and more as prostitutes and victims of sexual violence. In 2002 the Minneapolis, Minnesota–based advocacy group National Institute on Media and the Family issued its annual report card on video game content. That year the organization concentrated on what it perceived as an alarming trend of violence against women found in video games. The institute singled out the video game *Grand Theft Auto: Vice City* for criticism, pointing out that the game enables a player to score points by having sex with a prostitute, then killing her. Said the institute's report:

> *Grand Theft Auto: Vice City* is receiving rave reviews for its technical excellence. However, its portrayal and mistreatment of women is disturbing. The brutal murder of women as entertainment is cause for great concern. Parents of both boys and girls should be very alarmed by the following: Every day millions of boys and young men are entertaining themselves with a game that denigrates women and glamorizes violence against them. The theory that it is a game that only adults are playing is simply not valid. Our recent survey of boys showed that it is extremely popular with pre-teen and teen males.[15]

"Females may be as tough as the males, and may have to face similar missions and opponents, but they have an added challenge: to look sexy while doing it."[13]

— Children Now, a national advocacy group that studies trends and issues affecting children.

In 2005 parents' advocacy groups raised similar concerns about *Grand Theft Auto: San Andreas*, finding that the game features hidden sex scenes that players could unlock by downloading a software patch from the Internet. And in 2009 American retailers agreed to voluntarily ban sales of a Japanese-produced video game titled *RapeLay* that enables players to commit sexual violence against a female victim. Leigh Alexander, news editor of an online video game review site, found the game repugnant. "The interactive assaults are difficult to endure if you have a conscience,"[16] he said.

No Longer a Laughing Matter

Video games have come a long way since the days when players poured quarters into the *Pong* machine at Andy Capp's Tavern. Those simple and carefree days of game play have been replaced

Media watchdog and parent advocacy groups have singled out the Grand Theft Auto *series of games as featuring inappropriate sexual content, a hint of which can be seen in this image from the* Grand Theft Auto: San Andreas *version of the game.*

by a huge industry that employees thousands of developers, programmers, artists, and other highly skilled people to conjure up some truly exciting and cutting-edge entertainment. However, experts agree that video games have often taken players into the dark side—a fact that has been true since the first gremlins were plowed over by *Death Race* players. It could be suggested that given the simple graphics of the era, the violence found in *Death Race* was laughable. But in today's video game world, where the action on the screen is near lifelike, the murder of a virtual prostitute or rape of an innocent victim no longer seems like a laughing matter.

Facts

- The National Institute on Media and the Family reports that a third of the typical American family's entertainment budget is spent on video games.

- The Pew Internet & American Life Project found that 97 percent of all adolescents have played video games at least once in their lives.

- According to the Pew Internet & American Life Project, automobile racing games are the most popular games among Americans, with 74 percent preferring those games. Racing games are followed by puzzle-oriented games, 72 percent; sports games, 68 percent; and action-oriented games, 67 percent.

- A third of American parents play video games with their children at least some of the time.

- Eighty-one percent of adults between the ages of 18 and 29 play video games.

Do Violent Video Games Promote Real-Life Violence?

On a lazy summer night in 2003, 15-year-old Will Buckner and his 13-year-old stepbrother Josh traipsed through the brush near their home in Newport, Tennessee. They had taken their father's .22-caliber rifles. Now, crouched in the weeds overlooking the Interstate 40 highway, they started firing off rounds at cars and trucks as they sped by.

Earlier in the evening, the boys had been home in their basement, playing *Grand Theft Auto III*. It was Josh who came up with the idea: Instead of shooting at virtual cars, why not shoot at the real thing? Later, Will and Josh told police they had not intended to hurt anybody, they just wanted to see if they could hit the vehicles with their shots.

But their shots did hit people. Aaron Hamel and his cousin Denise Deneau were speeding along the interstate in Hamel's pickup truck when a shot pierced the vehicle's window, striking the 45-year-old man in the head. The truck quickly crashed into a guardrail. Kim Bede and her boyfriend, Marc Hickman, witnessed the crash. They were driving behind Hamel's vehicle, saw it go out of control, and assumed the vehicle had blown a tire. An instant later, a gunshot pierced the door of their car, striking Bede in the hip. When police arrived, they found Hamel dead and Bede seriously wounded.

The trail soon led police to the Buckner home, where the boys confessed to the shootings. Tried in juvenile court, Will and Josh pleaded guilty to reckless homicide and related charges. The judge found that they had not committed the shootings with murderous intent and sentenced them to a juvenile detention center. Under Tennessee law, since the crime was committed while they were juveniles, the boys were released when they reached the age of 19.

Clearly, the shootings were a tragedy, touching the lives of many individuals, including the two boys who must live with the memories of their crime for the rest of their lives. As to the cause of the tragedy, for most of the people involved there is little doubt. Says the boys' mother, Donna Buckner, "Will and Josh wouldn't have done this if they hadn't been playing that game. They aren't serial killers. They're good boys."[17]

Tragedy in Littleton

The first major incident that led many mental health experts to conclude that video game violence may be at the root of real-life violence occurred in 1999 in Littleton, Colorado, when high school seniors Dylan Klebold and Eric Harris opened fire on their classmates at Columbine High School, killing 13 others before taking their own lives. After the massacre, one fact about Klebold and Harris seemed to stand out: Both boys were avid players of the violent video games *Doom* and *Quake*.

In fact, the whole episode at Columbine High School had the eerie feeling of a video game, with Harris and Klebold acting as armed characters stalking through enemy terrain and mowing down anyone who crossed their paths. After the shootings, police discovered a videotape made by the two boys, in which they sipped whiskey, brandished their guns, and promised to kill as many as 250 Columbine students. At one point in the tape, Klebold even refers to *Doom*. "It's going to be like . . . *Doom*," Klebold predicts of the carnage to come. "Tick, tick, tick, tick. . . . Ha!"[18] Author and psychologist Gregory K. Moffatt, who studied the Columbine case, says Harris even altered his version of *Doom*, customizing the game so the victims could not fire back—exactly the way he expected to find students in the hallways and classrooms of Columbine High School. "[Harris] had computer modeled their crime by customizing the game *Doom* to make the shooters fight people

The Most Violent Games

Each year, Kym Worthy, prosecutor of Wayne County, Michigan, compiles a list of the 10 video games she regards as most violent. Worthy releases the list in late November as the holiday shopping season approaches so that parents know which games contain the most violent acts. "The last year has convinced me more than ever that children are at risk of becoming desensitized to violence and can exhibit more aggressive behavior if they repeatedly play certain violent video games," Worthy said as she released her 2008 list.

In recent years, games that have made Worthy's list include *Dead Space*, in which aliens kill their enemies by ripping off their limbs; *Gears of War 2*, which enables players to dispatch their enemies with chainsaws; *Saints Row 2*, a game that gives players opportunities to beat up strippers, shoot police officers, and slit the throats of rival gangsters; and *Call of Duty: Modern Warfare 2*, in which defenseless citizens at an airport are mowed down by the hero.

In 2007 Worthy's office won convictions against two teens, Jean Pierre Orlewicz and Alexander James Letkermann, who allegedly lured a victim to a garage, killed him with a knife, then mutilated the body. "The investigation revealed that the youths would often play violent video games," Worthy said. "I believe that certain video games are connected to the proliferation of violent crimes being committed by youthful offenders such as Orlewicz and Letkermann." Following their convictions, both youths were sentenced to lengthy prison terms.

Quoted in Ben Schmitt, "Prosecutor Worthy Cites Violent Video Games," *Detroit Free Press*, December 16, 2008. www.freep.com.

that could not fight back," says Moffatt. "It is amazing to me that any two adolescents could have kept such detailed plans secret for such a long time."[19]

In the years since the Columbine massacre, other incidents of real-life violence believed to have been prompted by video game play have surfaced in the headlines. In Oakland, California, several incidents of gang violence are believed to have been inspired by what gang members saw on their video game screens. In the Oakland case, members of a gang known as the Nut Cases played *Grand Theft Auto III*, then patterned their crimes after the violent acts they committed on-screen. During a 10-week crime spree in late 2002, 6 members of the gang are alleged to have committed 5 murders and dozens of robberies. Police eventually arrested all of the gang members. Gang leader Demarcus Ralls admitted to police, "The

Emergency personnel pull a student to safety during the 1999 Columbine High School shooting spree in Littleton, Colorado. Experts believe the two shooters, both avid players of violent video games, may have been influenced by the games.

people [we] shot did nothing to deserve it."[20] Ralls and other gang members were convicted and sentenced to life in prison.

In Fayette, Alabama, an avid 18-year-old *Grand Theft Auto: Vice City* player, Devin Moore, admitted to shooting two police officers and a police dispatcher, leading investigators to believe he was inspired by the action in the game. Willie Crump, whose son James was one of the police officers murdered by Moore, said, "Everything he did is right out of *Grand Theft Auto*. Why would you make a game like that to show kids how to kill cops?"[21] Moore—just 18 years old at the time of the crime—was convicted in the murders and sentenced to the death penalty.

Violence in TV and the Movies

The suggestion that images of violence in the media are responsible for promoting real-life violence did not begin with the development of *Doom* or the *Grand Theft Auto* series—or even with *Death Race* and *Custer's Revenge*. TV and movie producers have long heard similar complaints: that the violent action they depict on-screen has the potential to prompt some viewers to commit similar acts of violence in real life.

During the earliest days of TV, Popeye was ready to settle all arguments with his fists, while the Coyote's futile efforts to bag the Roadrunner usually ended when he found himself sailing head-first into a canyon wall. Meanwhile, during the 1960s and 1970s, following a series of court decisions that upheld the free speech rights of filmmakers, movie producers enjoyed new freedoms that enabled them to show graphic depictions of sex and violence on the screen. The fact that such violence-packed films as *The Wild Bunch*, *A Clockwork Orange*, *The Godfather*, and *Dirty Harry* drew huge audiences only solidified the notion among filmmakers that violence sells tickets at the box office.

As all this mayhem was unfolding on-screen, critics wondered whether the constant exposure to media violence was having an effect on the mental health of the viewers. "It's the emotionlessness of so many violent movies that I'm becoming anxious about," said *New Yorker* magazine film critic Pauline Kael. "There's something

"*Everything he did is right out of Grand Theft Auto. Why would you make a game like that to show kids how to kill cops?*"[21]

— Willie Crump, whose son James was one of the police officers murdered by Devin Moore.

deeply wrong about anyone's taking for granted the [effect on viewers] that this carnage without emotion represents."[22]

Over the years there have been many studies focusing on whether violence on TV and movie screens promotes real-life violence. In 2003 the American Psychological Association's journal, *Developmental Psychology*, released the results of a 15-year study in which the habits of 329 young people were monitored by mental health experts. The authors of the study first interviewed the participants when they were young children, monitoring their TV- and movie-viewing habits as they grew into young adults. At the conclusion of the study, the authors found:

> Men who were high TV-violence viewers as children were significantly more likely to have pushed, grabbed or shoved their spouses, to have responded to an insult by shoving a person, to have been convicted of a crime and to have committed a moving traffic violation. Such men, for example, had been convicted of crimes at over three times the rate of other men.
>
> Women who were high TV-violence viewers as children were more likely to have thrown something at their spouses, to have responded to someone who made them mad by shoving, punching, beating or choking the person, to have committed some type of criminal act, and to have committed a moving traffic violation. Such women, for example, reported having punched, beaten or choked another adult at over four times the rate of other women.[23]

Moreover, the authors of the study found a disturbing trend among participants—they preferred film and TV violence when it was perpetrated by the good guys or, at least, when the perpetrators were rewarded for committing violent acts. In the 1971 film *Dirty Harry*, for example, the tough San Francisco cop Harry Callahan, portrayed by Clint Eastwood, tracks a vicious killer whose acts are depicted on-screen. The authors of the study found that the viewers identified with the Callahan character and supported him even though he bent the law and used excessive violence to bring the killer to justice. In other words, the authors found, the

Video Games and the Prefrontal Cortex

The area of the brain that controls impulsive actions is known as the prefrontal cortex. Located just behind the forehead, the prefrontal cortex is one of the last areas of the brain to develop. In most people the prefrontal cortex is still under development past the age of 20. That is why teenagers often act impulsively—their prefrontal cortexes have not yet matured, preventing them from reacting to situations with calmness and reason.

Child psychologist David Walsh, the president of the National Institute on Media and the Family, says the manner in which Devin Moore committed three murders indicates that he acted impulsively. Moore had been arrested on suspicion of stealing a car. At the time, he had no criminal record. Inside the Fayette, Alabama, police station, Moore suddenly seized a police officer's gun and fired, killing the officer, another police officer, and a police dispatcher. It all happened within seconds.

Later, police learned that Moore was a dedicated *Grand Theft Auto* enthusiast, playing the game for hours each day. Clearly, Walsh says, the game implanted instructions in Moore's brain, prompting him to act impulsively and make the wrong decisions. Says Walsh, "When a young man with a developing brain, already angry, spends hours and hours and hours rehearsing violent acts, and then . . . he's put into a situation of emotional stress, there's a likelihood that he will literally go to that familiar pattern that's been wired repeatedly, perhaps thousands and thousands of times."

Quoted in *60 Minutes*, "Can a Video Game Lead to Murder?" CBS News, March 4, 2005. www.cbsnews.com.

young viewers were willing to accept violence as a way of life. Said the study:

> Violent scenes that children are most likely to model their behavior after are ones in which they identify with the perpetrator of the violence, the perpetrator is rewarded for the violence and in which children perceive the scene as telling about life like it really is. Thus, a violent act by someone like Dirty Harry that results in a criminal being eliminated and brings glory to Harry is of more concern than a bloodier murder by a despicable criminal who is brought to justice.[24]

The Desensitizing Effects of Media Violence

Not only do mental health experts find that viewers tend to support the perpetrators of TV and movie violence, but many experts also believe that constant exposure to simulated violence desensitizes the viewers to the real thing. In other words, seeing bodies explode in a shower of gunfire no longer provides much of a shock value to the viewer. Says author and University of Toronto psychology professor Jonathan L. Freedman:

> When people see a real act of violence, we hope they will respond with concern and do what they can to stop it. We want them to feel that violence is bad, that people should not commit violence, and that they themselves should never be violent. Most North Americans have witnessed few if any acts of real violence and have not had a chance to be desensitized to it. In contrast, they have witnessed a great many acts of violence in the media. If exposure to this media violence causes them to be less concerned about real violence, this would be almost as serious as if it caused them to commit violence themselves.[25]

Mental health experts find themselves particularly concerned about the desensitizing effects of video game violence. Indeed, many argue that the violence depicted in TV and the movies is far different than what the video game player experiences. The main difference, they argue, is the interactive nature of video game play. In TV and the movies, the viewer is merely somebody who is observing the action from the outside; in video games the player controls the action, firing the guns and blowing away his or her rivals.

A study by the Washington, D.C.–based Center for Media and Public Affairs found that levels of violence on TV and in the movies have actually been following a downward trend in recent years. The organization reported that between 1999 and 2001, the

Clint Eastwood's Dirty Harry *character (pictured) bends the law and uses excessive violence—all in the name of justice. Researchers have found that young viewers exposed to this type of violence come to accept it as natural.*

time devoted to depictions of violence on TV and film screens declined by 19 percent. On the other hand, the organization found, the amount of violence depicted in video games has been increasing. The study looked at 70 of the top-selling video games on the American market and found that no fewer than 89 percent contained depictions of violence. In addition, the study found that in 41 percent of the games, the players are *required* to use violence to achieve the goals of the games. In other words, to score points, murders or other acts of violence must be committed.

A report by the National Youth Violence Prevention Resource Center, an agency of the Centers for Disease Control and Prevention, concludes:

> The impact of the widespread use of violent video games is a cause of concern for researchers, because they fear that the interactive nature of video games may increase the likelihood of children learning aggressive behavior and that the increasing realism might encourage greater identification with characters and more imitation of the behaviors of video game models.[26]

Predispositions to Commit Violence

Not all experts agree with those conclusions. Some argue that violent video games do not prompt people into violent behavior unless they already have a predisposition to commit violence. Under those circumstances, they argue, it could take any type of trigger to prompt those persons into committing violent acts. "I don't think video games inspire people to commit crimes," insists Douglas Lowenstein, former president of the Entertainment Software Association, which represents game manufacturers. "If people have a criminal mind, it's not because they're getting their ideas from video games. There's something much more deeply wrong with the individual. And it's not the game that's the problem."[27]

Certainly, in some of the most celebrated cases of violence attributed to video game play, there is evidence to suggest that the perpetrators would have eventually committed violent acts with or without inspiration drawn from the games they played. In the

Columbine case, for example, there was clear evidence suggesting Harris and Klebold were both deeply troubled individuals. They harbored an unhealthy interest in Adolf Hitler, wearing clothes with Nazi-inspired insignia. Months before the shooting, Harris and Klebold were arrested for breaking into a van. At Columbine, they joined a group of social outcasts and misfits who called themselves the "Trench Coat Mafia"—as the name suggests, members dressed in black trench coats. The two boys were known to detest Columbine's student athletes. Sara Schweitzberger, a 15-year-old Columbine student, said she took a gym class with Klebold and could tell he was a troubled individual. "He really felt unloved," she said. "He wasn't so bad. He was lonely. I just wish I could give him a hug and tell him that I care."[28]

Likewise, in the Newport case, both boys harbored their own internal demons. Will was born slightly brain damaged, leaving him with below-normal intelligence. Josh's mother died when he was 11; he had also been diagnosed with a learning disability and had recently flunked the seventh grade. When the boys' parents married, it seemed both were heading for happier lives. But then an older stepbrother gave Josh *Grand Theft Auto III* for his birthday, and the game soon consumed both boys.

Donna Buckner admits to not understanding the violent nature of the game. "When I came downstairs, I'd just see them crashing in their cars," she says. "I didn't know you could kill prostitutes and stuff like that."[29] At one point, she admonished the boys, "You realize this is virtual reality, not reality?"[30] She recalls the boys nodded their heads, then went back to playing the game.

> "There's something deeply wrong about anyone's taking for granted the [effect on viewers] that this carnage without emotion represents."[22]
>
> — *New Yorker* magazine film critic Pauline Kael.

Scanning the Brains of Players

Although Buckner may not have realized it, *Grand Theft Auto III* was making an impression on the minds of her boys—and it is likely that they did not understand the game was only a game. In fact, there have been scientific studies that have determined the degree to which violent video games have stimulated parts of the brain.

At Indiana University School of Medicine, researchers took brain scans of teenagers after they played the games *Need for Speed:*

Underground and *Medal of Honor: Frontline.* Forty-four teenagers were drafted for the study. The researchers split the participants into two groups, assigning 22 to play *Need for Speed* and the other 22 to play *Medal of Honor.* All players were given 30 minutes of game time. Immediately after playing the games, the teenagers underwent magnetic resonance imaging, or MRI, tests, which produced images of their brains.

The MRI tests showed that in the 22 participants who played *Medal of Honor,* areas of the brain regulating emotions were stimulated. As for the teenagers who played *Need for Speed,* this effect was not present.

The researchers concluded that the differences in the test results could be attributed to the differences in the content of the games. *Need for Speed* is truly an exciting game—it is a racing game, with many thrilling moments requiring acceleration, driving skill, and race strategy. However, the game proceeds with little violent content. (The object of the game is to win the race, not to cause an opponent to crash.) On the other hand, the scenario of *Medal of Honor* finds the player taking the role of a commando fighting behind enemy lines during World War II. There is an abundance of violent content in the game as players blast away at enemy soldiers to accomplish their missions.

The results led the Indiana scientists to conclude that video games could prompt antisocial behavior, even among well-adjusted players. "There's enough data that clearly indicates that [game violence] is a problem," says Larry Ley, director of the Center for Successful Parenting, which funded the Indiana University study. "And it's not just a problem for kids with behavioral disorders."[31]

"When people see a real act of violence, we hope they will respond with concern and do what they can to stop it. We want them to feel that violence is bad, that people should not commit violence, and that they themselves should never be violent."[25]

— University of Toronto psychology professor Jonathan L. Freedman.

Juvenile Crime Declining

On the other hand, there are many experts who have yet to be convinced that video game violence leads players to commit violent acts away from their game consoles. Massachusetts Institute of Technology professor Henry Jenkins cites statistics that show the rate of violent crime committed by juveniles is at a 30-year low. In other words, he says, during the same era that saw the rise in popularity of such games as *Death Race, Mortal Kombat, Doom,* and *Grand Theft*

Auto, the number of violent crimes committed by young people had been following a downward trend. Given the fact that nearly all teenage boys and about half of all teenage girls play video games regularly, Jenkins says, it is obvious that the vast majority of teenage players are able to leave the emotions of participating in the game behind when the game is over.

Moreover, he says, sociologists have studied the types of activities in which young offenders participate directly before they commit crimes, and have found that very few of them are reading books, watching TV or movies, or playing video games. Therefore, he says, it is clear that a young offender is not sitting on his or her couch, playing *Grand Theft Auto*, and is then suddenly prompted to find a prostitute to kill or a bank to rob. "No research has found that video games are a primary factor or that violent video game play could turn an otherwise normal person into a killer,"[32] Jenkins insists.

Jenkins says young people who commit violent acts usually have troubled lives at home. He suggests authorities would do well to address those types of issues rather than focus on the content of the games young people play. "The moral panic over violent video games is doubly harmful," says Jenkins. "It has led adult authorities to be more suspicious and hostile to many kids who already feel cut off from the system. It also misdirects energy away from eliminating the actual causes of youth violence and allows problems to fester."[33]

> *"I don't think video games inspire people to commit crimes. If people have a criminal mind, it's not because they're getting their ideas from video games."*[27]
>
> — Douglas Lowenstein, former president of the Entertainment Software Association.

There Will Always Be Violent People

Certainly, violent video games are an easy target. In both the Columbine and Newport cases, evidence surfaced linking the perpetrators with violent video game play. Eric Harris was so wrapped up in his game play that he posted comments on the Internet, explaining how he mastered *Doom* and *Quake*. He also possessed some computer savvy, enabling him to alter the games and create new levels of competition. Meanwhile, shortly after his arrest for three murders, Devin Moore told police, "Life is like a video game. Everybody's got to die sometime."[34]

Regardless of that evidence, many mental health experts are convinced that it takes more than a fondness for controlling virtual acts of violence to prompt somebody actually to go out and commit real acts of violence. They suggest that there will always be violent people, and it just so happens that some of them also enjoy playing video games.

Facts

- A study published in the journal *Pediatrics and Adolescent Medicine* found that young males who play *Grand Theft Auto III* exhibit high blood pressure readings while playing. High blood pressure is often regarded as an indication of stress.

- At Iowa State University, a study of 210 students found that participants who played the violent video game *Wolfenstein 3D* acted more aggressively after the game than students who played the nonviolent game *Myst*.

- In 2008 *Grand Theft Auto IV* sold more copies on the first day of its release than any other video game in history; the game sold 3.6 million copies, earning its developer profits of more than $300 million.

- The judge who found 17-year-old Daniel Petric guilty of killing his father said the boy fully expected the man to get up, unharmed, after he shot him in the head. Petric, of Wellington, Ohio, was a dedicated fan of the violent video game *Halo 3*.

- A study of nearly 3,000 video game players by Rochester University in New York concluded that it was the challenge of mastering the games, rather than the violent content of the games, that interested the players the most.

- A study of 430 American students in the third through fifth grades found that children who play violent video games early in the school year develop behavioral problems by late in the school year. Companion studies in Germany, Finland, and Japan produced similar results.

Do Video Games Lead to Addiction and Social Isolation?

Shawn Woolley discovered the online video game *EverQuest* at the age of 20, and within a year it had consumed his life. Woolley became so engrossed in the game that he quit his job and did little else but sit alone in his apartment in front of the computer screen, playing the fantasy role-playing game. On Thanksgiving morning in 2001, Woolley's mother, Liz Woolley, discovered his body. Her son had committed suicide, shooting himself while sitting in front of his computer screen. It was clear that he had been playing *EverQuest*—the game was still on the screen when his body was found. "He couldn't stay off it," Liz Woolley said. "That's how strong that game is. You can't just get up and walk away."[35]

Most *EverQuest* players would agree—some refer to the game as *EverCrack*, believing it as addictive as crack cocaine. Other games are equally addictive, if not more so, leading many sociologists and psychologists to voice concerns about the social isolation that is often created by video game addiction. "Time becomes irrelevant," says David Walsh of the National Institute on Media and the Family. "For some people, this is the center of their lives."[36]

When people do little else but sit at home playing video games, they do not make or keep friends, they do not learn how to interact with others face-to-face, they may lose interest in school and work, and they have no interest in starting families. If they already have families, they may spend little time with spouses and children. Sherry Myrow of Toronto, Canada, says her husband would eat and sleep little as he spent 18 hours a day playing video games. "I only saw happiness in his eyes if he was playing the game or talking about the game," she says. "The game consumed his life, and there was no room for me."[37] Myrow's husband suffered from what could be diagnosed as an addiction to video games.

What Is Addiction?

According to the American Psychiatric Association, addiction is defined as the loss of control over the use of a substance, such as alcohol or drugs, as well as the inability to stop despite negative consequences. However, addiction does not have to be prompted by the use of a substance; it is also defined as a loss of control over a pattern of behavior. Says Joseph Frascella, director of the division of clinical neuroscience at the National Institute on Drug Abuse, "Addictions are repetitive behaviors in the face of negative

On-Line Gamers Anonymous (background) offers support to those affected by gaming addiction. Pictured is one member of the group whose son underwent dramatic changes as a result of video game addiction.

consequences, the desire to continue something you know is bad for you."[38]

The most common forms of addiction are to drugs or alcohol. These are physical dependencies that can find their roots in the interaction of the chemical composition of the substances with an area in the central portion of the brain known as the ventral tegmentum. This is the pleasure center of the brain. When the ventral tegmentum is stimulated, it provides the body with pleasurable feelings.

This area of the brain is rich in chemicals known as neurotransmitters, which carry messages from brain cell to brain cell. Among the neurotransmitters found in this area of the brain are dopamine, serotonin, norepinephrine, and endorphin. These neurotransmitters affect emotions. When drugs or alcoholic beverages are consumed, they enter the bloodstream and soon interact with neurotransmitters in the brain, either enhancing their flow or reducing their flow, which affects the user's emotions. That explains why drinkers and drug users are often happy, giddy, or euphoric.

If the user continues abusing drugs or alcohol, he or she could develop a physical craving—the body demands the substances that stimulate the brain's pleasure center. That person is now addicted to drugs or alcohol. Although not regarded as drug abusers, cigarette smokers may also find themselves with chemical-based addictions because the chemicals in tobacco could also prompt physical cravings in the body.

There are other forms of addictions. People can suffer addictions to gambling and sex. Some people find work addictive. Others are shopaholics. For some people, food can be addictive. Some people are actually addicted to housework. Mental health experts have concluded these activities could also stimulate the ventral tegmentum even though no chemical influences are involved.

> "I only saw happiness in his eyes if he was playing the game or talking about the game. The game consumed his life, and there was no room for me."[37]
>
> — Sherry Myrow, wife of a video game addict.

Addicted to Gaming

Many mental health experts believe video game play can also turn into addictive behavior. Hilarie Cash, a psychotherapist in Redmond, Washington, treats patients with addictive behaviors and says many of her clients are addicted to video games. She says:

I see it in my clients. . . . These [clients] I'm working with—the majority of them are young men. And they come in, they have lost jobs, lost marriages, dropped out of college or high school, and their lives have fallen apart. They exhibit all of the standard characteristics. Their behavior is compulsive, they get a high off of it, they do it in spite of negative consequences.[39]

Most substance abusers start out small—a drink here or a drink there, or they may experiment with small quantities of drugs. After a time, they find they need more than one drink or several doses of drugs to achieve a satisfying high. Soon it takes large quantities of drugs or alcohol to satisfy their desires. According to Cash, many of her clients exhibit symptoms similar to people she has seen who are addicted to drugs and alcohol. "People will play . . . an hour of *World of Warcraft*, let's say, but then, after that, it's no longer making them high. They want more. And so they play more. And they develop tolerance over time. . . . Just over a matter of weeks and months, people can end up with a severe addiction."[40]

When Games Interfere with Real Life

Clearly, Woolley fit the description of someone suffering from an addiction. In Woolley's case his addiction led him into self-destructive behavior. Sadly, the Woolley case is not an isolated incident. Most video game addicts do not take their own lives, but there is abundant evidence that would suggest their addictions have interfered with their lives.

In Roxbury, Massachusetts, a mother woke one morning at 2:30 A.M. to find her 14-year-old son playing *Grand Theft Auto*. When he refused to turn off the PlayStation and go to bed, she called the police—it was the only way she could convince him to stop playing the game. "That she went to the extreme of calling the police tells me more about her level of frustration than anything else,"[41] says psychologist Lawrence Kutner.

Going Through Withdrawal

In South Carolina, a 21-year-old student named Ruya developed an addiction to *World of Warcraft*. The game, played on the Inter-

How to Tell If a Video Game Player Is Addicted

The National Institute on Media and the Family has identified certain attitudes and behaviors that may signal video game addiction. Some of these include:

- Video game use produces intense feelings of pleasure or guilt.
- Players think about the games even when they are not playing them.
- Hours of video game play increase over time, disrupting family life, schoolwork, employment, and social life.
- People lie about their video game habits, usually telling others they do not play very often or for very long periods of time.
- When not playing games, people feel such withdrawal symptoms as anger and depression.
- People would rather play games, particularly Internet-based games, than share time with spouses or friends.
- Players find their wrists are sore; they also do not sleep well and may suffer from dry eyes.
- Players neglect personal hygiene or skip meals.

net, requires players to assume the roles of characters who dwell in the mystical world of Azeroth, populated by trolls, dragons, and other mythological creatures. Ruya assumed the identity of a blue-haired elf. "The elf was everything I wasn't, everything I wanted to be," Ruya says. "Her world was as exciting as mine was boring."[42]

At first Ruya played occasionally, but she eventually found herself playing as much as 20 hours a week, immersed in the world of Azeroth. Soon *World of Warcraft* turned into Ruya's whole world—she dropped out of school, stopped seeing friends and family members, gained weight, and even stopped bathing.

"When I wasn't playing *World of Warcraft*, I would get fidgety," she says. "It's all I would talk about. I used to hate vacations because that meant time away from *World of Warcraft*."[43]

Any drug and alcohol abuser knows what happens when he or she suddenly stops using the substances. The body, no longer receiving the chemicals that satisfy the pleasure center of the brain, goes through withdrawal. Symptoms vary, but most addicts experience nausea, vomiting, sweating, shakiness, and anxiety. Depending on the nature of the addiction, symptoms can last a few days or a few weeks.

In Ruya's case she finally realized what had happened to her life—that *World of Warcraft* had taken over. Ruya resolved to kick her video game habit, so she uninstalled the game from her computer—and soon found herself going through withdrawal symptoms. At first she developed bad headaches. Next she grew depressed and tried to take her own life by overdosing on sleeping pills—the effort failed when her mother intervened. With the help of her parents, Ruya sought professional counseling and was able to beat her addiction to *World of Warcraft*. "At least I am a person now, not an elf," she says. "I'm working on staying grounded in the real world."[44]

"These [clients] I'm working with—the majority of them are young men. And they come in, they have lost jobs, lost marriages, dropped out of college or high school, and their lives have fallen apart."[39]

— Psychotherapist Hilarie Cash.

Video Games Can Be Socially Isolating

Mental health experts have started looking into cases like Ruya's with an eye toward seeing the type of long-term and short-term effects that might be prompted by addiction to video games. A 2009 study conducted at Brigham Young University in Utah looked at the video game habits of more than 800 college students and found that students who spend the most time playing video games have the most difficulty in maintaining relationships with peers.

The authors of the study found that video game play can definitely be socially isolating—cutting people off from many other normal activities of life. Indeed, the study suggested that people who spend several hours each day concentrating on their video game play miss out on opportunities to be with friends, sharing good times. Likewise, the authors suggested, some people who may find themselves uncomfortable in social settings may retreat to the virtual worlds of video games, where they can assume the roles of self-assured, heroic characters. In other words, they lose themselves in the fantasy worlds of their games. Said Brigham Young psychology professor Laura Walker, "It may be that young adults remove themselves from important social settings to play video games, or that people who already struggle with relationships are trying to find other ways to spend their time. My guess is that it's some of both."[45]

Male students were found to be more addicted to games than female students. The authors determined that male students played video games four times as much as females. The authors suggested that this statistic may have far-reaching implications. Would men damage their relationships with their wives and girlfriends by spending too much time playing video games? Said Brigham Young student Alex Jensen, who helped author the study, "The gender imbalance begs the question of whether chasing a new high score beats spending quality time with a girlfriend or wife."[46]

Moreover, the study found, students who play video games daily smoke marijuana twice as much as casual players and three times more than students who never play video games. The study also found that female students who admit to addictions to video games suffer from low self-esteem. Concluded Walker, "Everything we found associated with video games came out negative."[47]

> "It may be that young adults remove themselves from important social settings to play video games, or that people who already struggle with relationships are trying to find other ways to spend their time."[45]
> — Brigham Young psychology professor Laura Walker.

MMORPGs: The Most Addictive Games

Both Woolley and Ruya were addicted to what are known as "massively multiplayer online role-playing games" or MMORPGs. In these games, which include *EverQuest* and *World of Warcraft*, thousands of players who are connected through the Internet participate at the same time, sharing in the fantasies of playing roles in make-believe worlds. These games provide them with a sense of belonging to a community, although in this case it is a virtual community. People make no face-to-face contact, and they know each other only as elves, knights, or other mythical beings.

And there is no question that they are truly addictive. In South Korea, for example, a 28-year-old man was found slumped

The Gamer Widows

Soon after her wedding, Sherry Myrow of Toronto, Ontario, discovered her husband's addiction to playing online games. After enduring months of loneliness while her husband was glued to his computer screen, Myrow decided to do something about it. She established the Web site Gamer Widow, an online forum for wives and husbands in similar situations to vent their frustrations and also share ideas on how to wean their spouses away from the games.

Soon after the site went live, it drew some 500 members. Myrow believes it has been instrumental in saving at least two marriages. "In both cases," Myrow says, "the gamer widow showed the site to their gamer, and together [they] worked through their problems."

As for Myrow, she took some of the advice that other gamer widows posted on the site. She started playing the game alongside her husband so that she could develop a deeper understanding of the gaming experience. In time she was able to convince her husband that certain situations involving his character were not worth the time away from his family. "A gamer has to be OK with letting his hero die when his loved one needs him," Myrow says. "The first time my husband was completely OK with letting his character [die] was momentous for me. I felt important and special, and I had no problem with him playing for another four hours."

Quoted in *Computer Gaming World*, "+5 Band of Marital Bliss," March 2006, p. 39.

over his computer, dead, after spending what may have been seven days straight playing the MMORPG *StarCraft* in an Internet café. Witnesses reported seeing the man taking breaks only to go to the bathroom—they believe he ate little and did not sleep the entire week. "We presume the cause of death was heart failure stemming from exhaustion,"[48] said a police official in the province of Taegu.

A 15-year-old boy in Sweden suffered an epileptic convulsion after playing *World of Warcraft* with his friends for 24 hours straight. "They played all day and all night," the boy's father told reporters. "Maybe they got a few hours of sleep. They ate a little food and breakfast at their computers."[49]

Mental health experts report that these cases are not unusual. They often see clients who admit to spending all day engrossed in their MMORPG worlds. Says Richard Graham, a London, England, child psychiatrist:

> Some of my clients will discuss playing games for 14 to 16 hours a day at times without breaks and for those [clients] the consequences are potentially severe.
>
> The problem with *World of Warcraft* is the degree it can impact and create a socially withdrawn figure who may be connecting with people in the game and is largely dropping out of education [and] social opportunities.[50]

According to psychologist Mark Griffiths of Nottingham, England, a major difference between an MMORPG and a video game one would play on a console is that the MMORPG requires much more time—the player simply cannot walk away after just 20 or 30 minutes of play. In an MMORPG game, the puzzles and mysteries offered to the player often take hours to unravel. In contrast, in a typical console game, the player can boot up the game, spend 20 or 30 minutes blasting away at targets, and then find something else to do. "[MMORPGs] are the type of games that completely engross the player," says Griffiths. "They are not games that you can play for 20 minutes and stop. If you are going to take it seriously, you have to spend time doing it."[51]

Playing Video Games Together

Despite the feelings of such experts as Graham, Griffiths, and Cash, many mental health professionals do not accept the concept of video game addiction. And rather than accept the notion that video games are socially isolating, these professionals insist the opposite: that video games have the power to draw people together.

Indeed, some studies have found that, rather than leading to social isolation, video game play often enhances a sense of community among players and actually makes them more out-going and comfortable among others. This is true mostly among young people—playing video games seems to be just another activity that most teenagers do together. They may already go to fast-food restaurants together, play basketball together, and attend cheerleading practice together. Now, video game playing can be added to the list of activities teenagers do together.

In fact, a 2008 study by the Pew Internet & American Life Project found that 65 percent of teenagers play video games with friends or family members. The study also found that 82 percent of teenagers do play games by themselves, but 71 percent of those players also play with others. Therefore, teenagers who strictly play alone are a minority. Said the Pew study:

> For most teens, gaming is a social activity and a major com-ponent of their overall social experience. Teens play games in a variety of ways, including with others in person, with others online, and by themselves. Although most teens play games by themselves at least occasionally, just [some] teens only play games alone, and the remaining . . . teens play games with others at least some of the time.[52]

The multiplayer online role-playing game World of Warcraft *connects thousands of players, including these two people in a virtual community of elves, knights, and other mythical beings. Games such as this can be extremely addictive.*

Moreover, the study found, young people who play video games are as interested in current events as young people who either do not play games or spend little of their time at the game console. The study found that gamers often participate in charitable functions and are otherwise engaged in civic life. "The quantity of game play is not strongly related (positively or negatively) to most indicators of teens' interest and engagement in civil and social activity," said the Pew report. "For all . . . indicators of civic and political engagement, there were no significant differences between teens who play games every day and teens who play less than once a week."[53]

Dark and Troubling Ideas

Some mental health experts point out that even though video games have been a part of American life since the 1970s—and the social and psychological impacts of game playing have been studied for many years—so-called video game addiction is still not regarded as a legitimate physical or mental illness. In contrast, they point out, drug and alcohol addictions are considered true illnesses with established treatment programs available to patients. "It is important to note that there is currently no such clinical criteria as video game 'addiction' that has been accepted by any reputable organization for defining disorders of the mind or body,"[54] insists Richard T.A. Wood, a psychology professor at Nottingham Trent University in England.

Rob Cover, a professor of media theory at Victoria University in New Zealand, says addiction to video games can hardly be regarded in the same context as addiction to drugs and alcohol, which are true addictions that can be diagnosed through psychiatric and medical tests. Moreover, he suggests that people who believe video games can be addictive probably do not spend a lot of time playing them, and therefore they have conjured up dark and troubling ideas about the games drawn from popular culture. Cover says:

Popular concerns that children are now playing digital games rather than reading, or playing with "physical" toys such as building blocks or footballs, are voiced often by

"The problem with World of Warcraft is the degree it can impact and create a socially withdrawn figure who may be connecting with people in the game and is largely dropping out of education [and] social opportunities."[50]

— Child psychiatrist Richard Graham.

opinion-makers and politicians. . . . Games are seen as addictive not because of an inherent feature in particular games or among particular players but because gaming is viewed as an activity of choice of youth and [is regarded] as the chief entry to a world seen as dangerous, unknown, unknowable, virtual and drug-like.[55]

Cover suggests people who spend a great deal of time playing video games are no more addicted or socially isolated than those who spend equal amounts of time watching TV, reading books, or solving crossword puzzles. "Television can be watched for an entire day, whether stationary on one channel or zapped endlessly for hours," says Cover. "A book can be read with few breaks throughout the night. And like electronic games, they invoke a particular imaginary space."[56]

The positions taken by experts like Cover and Wood are endorsed by officials of the video game industry, who contend that their games are not addictive or socially isolating. Shortly after the death of Shawn Woolley, John Smedley, the chief executive officer of Sony Online, the developer of *EverQuest*, said he contacted Liz Woolley. Said Smedley, "When I spoke with Ms. Woolley, I expressed my condolences. And it's really one of those terrible things that happens. And there's just nothing to suggest that *EverQuest* had any role in his death. *EverQuest* is a game. And I don't see any connection between a form of entertainment and somebody's tragic suicide."[57]

Unable to Walk Away

Those words were probably not very satisfying to Liz Woolley or to the family of the South Korean *StarCraft* player who collapsed and died after spending a week staring at his screen. Certainly, there are enough former video game addicts who have been fortunate in that they have kicked their addictions and are now willing to talk about the experiences of living only for their games—not eating regularly, not sleeping regularly, neglecting personal hygiene, ignoring friends and family members. "Before [*World of Warcraft*], I had a job," says Ruya. "I worked out every day. I kept my room clean. I got my nails and hair done. I took care of myself. That all changed when I became addicted."[58]

Many video game players are able to walk away from their games, treating them as nothing more than light entertainment. It is also true, however, that many cannot.

Facts

- A Washington, D.C.–based market research firm found that 80 percent of parents who own video game systems play the games with their children, and two-thirds of gamer parents believe the experiences draw their families closer together.

- A study by the Kaiser Family Foundation found that 49 percent of gamers between the ages of 8 and 18 have video game consoles in their bedrooms, which are often places where they can seek privacy from parents and others.

- A study published in the journal *Cyber Psychology and Behavior* found that 12 percent of all gamers fit the diagnostic criteria for addiction established by the American Psychiatric Association.

- *The International Journal of Mental Health and Addiction* reported the results of a study that found the most likely reason that people play video games excessively is they possess poor time management skills. Another widespread reason is their desire to seek escape from their problems, the journal reported.

- A study of 64 young online gamers in China and Taiwan found that it did not matter whether the gamers were new to the experience or veteran players, most lost track of time and had difficulty breaking off their gaming experiences.

- Syracuse University studied 100 players of massively multiplayer online role-playing games and found that for the most part, such players suffer from poorer overall health, poorer quality of sleep, and more difficulty socializing with others than people who do not play those games.

Do Young Gamers Risk Their Health and Well-Being?

As a dedicated player of *World of Warcraft*, Brian Alegre often allowed himself no more than 30 seconds for a bathroom break before rushing back to the game. It was not unusual for the teenager from Westminster, California, to play for 15 or 20 hours a day during the summer. During the school year, Alegre played a bit less, but still spent most of his free time in front of his computer screen.

Alegre finally learned about the harm he was doing to himself when, three weeks before his high school senior project was due, he suddenly realized he had not even started work on the project. Unless he completed his senior project on time, Alegre knew he would not graduate. "I had a whole year to do my senior project, which is a requirement to graduate, but I was too busy playing the game," Alegre says. "So three weeks before it was due, I quit cold turkey."[59]

The student managed to finish his project on time and did go on to graduate. Alegre has learned his lesson. He has not given up playing video games, but now spends much less time at the screen—no more than two hours a night. Now he finds himself spending more of his free time playing tennis and sharing activities with friends and family members.

Alegre's case is not unique—many young people are known to neglect their studies because taking time to read books or practice for math tests means spending less time at their video game consoles. For many students, even though it means poor grades in school, giving up their time playing video games is not a sacrifice they are willing to make. Says Iowa State University professor Douglas A. Gentile, who has studied the impact of video game play on school performance, "For every hour a child is in front of a screen, he is not reading, exploring, creating or doing any number of other things that might have a long-term benefit."[60]

Neglecting Homework for Video Games

There are many studies that have assessed the effect of video game play on academic performance, and most have concluded what Alegre found out—that a devotion to gaming often adversely affects the quality of schoolwork performed by students. For example, a study by Argosy University's Minnesota School on Professional Psychology tracked the grades and video game playing habits of more than 600 eighth- and ninth-grade students and found that video game addicts argue a lot with their teachers, fight a lot with their friends, and score lower grades than others who play video games less often.

For example, the study found that nearly 5 percent of addicted video gamers are failing their school courses, while less than 1 percent of nonaddicted gamers are failing their courses. (For the purposes of the Argosy University study, addicted video game players were identified as those who play more than 24 hours a week.) On the other end of the spectrum, the study found that 25 percent of nonaddicted gamers carry A averages in school, while about 10 percent of addicted gamers could be considered A students.

Moreover, a study coauthored by Gentile at Iowa State University questioned 1,178 video game players between the ages of 8 and 18 about their playing habits, and found that 23 percent routinely skip their homework to play games, while 19 percent occasionally skip their homework to spend time at their video game consoles. In addition, 20 percent of the students admitted that their video game habits are often responsible for poor grades on tests or school assignments, while 12 percent admitted that playing video games has occasionally been responsible for poor grades.

"I had a whole year to do my senior project, which is a requirement to graduate, but I was too busy playing the game. So three weeks before it was due, I quit cold turkey."[59]

— Brian Alegre, a California student whose video game play nearly kept him from graduating high school.

These studies do not show that all avid video gamers are heading for academic failure, nor do they prove that to be an A student, a young person must limit his or her video game playing time. Nevertheless, these studies illustrate that students who spend a lot of their time in front of their game consoles have found it more difficult to maintain high averages in school than others who restrict their playing time. The studies also show that addicted players have provided themselves with more opportunities to fail. "The addicted group revealed more reports of involvement in physical fights in the last year, more arguments with friends and teachers, high [hostility], and lower grades," wrote Gentile and coauthor Marny R. Hauge. "These results suggest that video game addiction . . . is associated with adjustment problems such as school performance and aggressive attitudes and behaviors."[61]

Certainly, it does not take a psychologist to get to the root of the problem. If a young person is spending 24 hours or more a week playing video games, then he or she has less time to study adequately for a math test, or write a research paper, or read a book for a book report.

Squeezing Out Homework

Dating back to the 1950s and 1960s, parents and educators heard similar concerns about children who spent too much time watching TV, but the problem seems to have taken on added weight in recent years due to the growing popularity of video games as well as the Internet. Now, it seems, many young people continue to watch TV, but they are also finding ways to squeeze in time to play video games while spending hours on Facebook and texting one another. Something has to suffer, and in many cases what suffers is schoolwork.

A report by the Kaiser Family Foundation, a Menlo Park, California, organization that studies public health issues, tracked the habits of 2,000 students in the second through twelfth grades, finding that they spend an average of 6.5 hours a day engaged by media, which includes watching TV and DVDs as well as spending time on the Internet and playing video games. In other words, many young people spend nearly 46 hours a week staring at a

What Do Video Games Teach?

Video games can teach more than just hand-eye coordination. According to James Paul Gee, a professor of reading at the University of Wisconsin, games teach players the benefits of taking risks, how to respond to challenges, how to explore and rethink goals, and how to respond to frustration. "Good games stay within, but at the outer edge, of the player's 'regime of competence,'" says Gee. "That is, [games] feel doable but challenging. This stage is highly motivating for learners. School is often too easy for some students and too hard for others, even in the same classroom."

According to Gee, games also teach problem-solving skills. In the typical game, Gee says, the first problems are easy to solve, but as the game progresses, the nature of the problems grows more complex. Gee says he never played a video game until he played alongside his young son, Sam. When he saw how well Sam responded to the game, Gee decided to explore further, so he obtained the game *The New Adventures of the Time Machine* and played on his own. "As I confronted the game, I was amazed," Gee says. "All of my Baby-Boomer ways of learning and thinking did not work, and I felt myself using learning muscles that had not had this much of a workout since my graduate school days."

James Paul Gee, "Good Video Games and Good Learning," *Phi Kappa Phi Forum*, Summer 2005.

screen, mostly for entertainment rather than educational purposes. Says Victoria Rideout, an author of the Kaiser study and director of the organization's Program for the Study of Entertainment Media and Health:

We did find a strong negative relationship between the amount of time that kids spend with media and the type of grades that they report getting. So we classified kids into different categories of heavy, medium and light media users based on the amount of time they spend with media each day. And among the light media users, about a quarter of them say they usually get fair or poor grades—C's or below. Among the heavy media users, about half of them say they usually get those types of grades.[62]

Gentile says a reason grades may suffer is students often try to do their homework while engaged with the TV, the Internet, and even while playing video games. "As media dominates our lives, you can see it in our living rooms, where we often have a shrine to electronics,"[63] he says.

Indeed, some mental health experts have examined the ability of students to absorb important information while they are distracted by TV, the Internet, and video games. At the University of Michigan, psychologists asked adult volunteers to solve math problems while they were occasionally distracted by images and shapes—the type that might flash across a video game screen. As expected, the more the volunteers were distracted, the more mistakes they made. Says Patricia Greenfield, director of the Children's Digital Media Center at the University of California at Los Angeles, "Kids are getting better at paying attention to several things at once, but there is a cost in that you don't go into any one thing in as much depth."[64]

Prohibiting Video Games

Despite the overwhelming evidence that points toward the adverse effects video game play may have on academic performance, few educators believe the way to solve the problem is by prohibiting video game play by students. Most educators realize that would be a futile strategy—after all, schools have never had the ability to monitor how students spend their leisure time.

Parents can keep watch over the video game habits of their sons and daughters, but educators also recognize the limited influence many parents may exert on children, particularly older children. In many homes, both parents work, which means they are not home in the afternoons when students arrive home from school and boot up their video game consoles. Gentile adds that many parents make the mistake of letting their children have TV sets in their bedrooms. He suggests that when parents send their sons and daughters upstairs after dinner to do their homework, there is always the danger that the students will instead turn on their TVs and insert their favorite video games into their consoles. "If [they] have a TV in the bedroom, you are less able to monitor what your children are watching," he says. "You are more likely to have bad grades in school."[65]

Using Games to Teach

Many experts have recognized that video games and similar distractions are a fact of life in the 2010s and have proposed that teachers find ways to use video games for instructional purposes. In fact, some schools have designed video games into their curricula—not games like *Gears of War*, certainly, but educational games designed to help students learn about math, physics, and other subjects. Edward O. Wilson, a Harvard University biology professor who has advanced theories on human evolution, believes games could be designed to provide students with virtual looks back into history, showing them different stages of the development of the planet. "Games are the future in education," insists Wilson. "I envision visits to different ecosystems that the student could actually enter . . . with an instructor. They could [see] a rain forest, a tundra, or a Jurassic forest."[66]

One of the first schools to make gaming a big part of its curriculum is Quest to Learn, an experimental middle school in New York City. At the school, sixth-grade students take their seats in their classroom at video game monitors, then spend time playing *Little Big Planet*. The game helps players learn how to create and manipulate shapes and has been given high marks by educators for teaching the principles of physics. In another class, art students learn the techniques of design through a game titled *Gamestar Mechanic*. In another classroom, students play a game that enables them to assume roles as location scouts for mock TV reality shows—by playing the game, the students must research different climate zones and create maps. "Students now live to play games and are immersed in technology," says Ginger Stevens, a Quest to Learn teacher. "It makes sense to tap into that enthusiasm. Instead of enforcing an old model of education for them, we're looking at where students are coming from and building a program around that."[67]

"Kids are getting better at paying attention to several things at once, but there is a cost in that you don't go into any one thing in as much depth."[64]

— Patricia Greenfield, director of the Children's Digital Media Center at the University of California at Los Angeles.

Encouraging Employees to Play Games

Some high-tech firms encourage their employees to take time out from work to play games at their office computers. At JotSpot, a software company near San Francisco, company owner Joe Kraus says the games give his employees opportunities to relax from their high-pressure jobs. Most employees, he says, prefer adventure-oriented games. "People are pretty amazed when I tell them I take my entire engineering staff offline for 30 to 40 minutes to do this," says Kraus.

Other high-tech firms encourage employees to engage in online role-playing games such as *World of Warcraft*. Executives believe that when employees play together, they learn team-building concepts that they can later use in their professional roles. Says Douglas Thomas, a communications professor at the University of Southern California in Los Angeles:

> There's a quote from Plato that [says] you learn more about a person in an hour of play than in a lifetime of conversation. And there really is something to that. You see people at their best and at their worst. You get to see how they deal with adversity. You work as a group to overcome incredible challenges. You forge very powerful connections very quickly by overcoming obstacles.

Quoted in Jessica Guynn, "Making Gaming Pay Off," *San Francisco Chronicle*, July 23, 2006, p. F-1.

Parents seem satisfied. Lesli Baker, the mother of an 11-year-old Quest to Learn student, says her son struggled in other public schools, mostly because the child suffers from attention deficit disorder, a learning disability that makes the boy hyperactive, impulsive, and unable at times to concentrate. According to Baker, the games seem to hold his attention better than his teachers have. "It's a great match for him," Baker says. "He's really enthused about learning."[68]

Other schools are also finding ways to incorporate video game play into their curricula. Many educators say they are convinced that old-style classrooms that feature little more than blackboards and books will not meet the needs of young people who are growing up in a digital age. School planners realize they will have to wire classrooms to the Internet and provide them with resources that will hold the attention of students. Some of those resources are likely to include video games. Says Stan Goldberg, an education professor at San Francisco State University in California, "If you look at many classrooms, they are dull, they are boring and they are not very educational. If children are given [the choice of] an uninteresting classroom and a video game, there is no question they will go for the video game."[69]

Video Games and Obesity

Many educators may find themselves in support of the notion that video game play should be incorporated into school curricula, but chances are that few would suggest that sports-oriented games like *Madden NFL* or *Tiger Woods PGA Tour* should replace gym classes. In fact, many educators and other experts are concerned about video game play leading to obesity. As young people sit on their sofas playing video games or are engaged with other forms of electronic media, they certainly are not outdoors playing sports or otherwise getting exercise. And not only are they sitting at home and not getting exercise, but chances are that many of them are eating fatty snack foods while they are playing video games.

Obesity can be a serious condition. An obese person is defined by the National Institutes of Health as somebody who is at least 30 pounds (13.6kg) overweight, the point at which excess body weight becomes a health hazard. Obese people face a number of risks, such as heart disease, diabetes, arthritis in joints, high blood pressure, and sleep apnea, a condition in which the extra weight of the neck presses down on the windpipe, interrupting sleep and potentially causing choking. About 300,000 people a year die from illnesses related to obesity.

According to the American Heart Association, more than 9 million children and adolescents between the ages of 6 and 19 are

"Students now live to play games and are immersed in technology. It makes sense to tap into that enthusiasm."[67]

— Quest to Learn teacher Ginger Stevens.

considered overweight or obese. That number is triple the estimated number of overweight and obese young people in 1980—or about the time video game use started to become widespread. Is it any wonder why? A 150-pound person (68kg) who sits on the sofa playing video games for half an hour will burn 53 calories. If that same person spends half an hour playing basketball, he or she would burn 280 calories. Says U.S. Representative John Sarbanes of Maryland, whose congressional committee has examined the reasons for childhood obesity:

> Research . . . indicates that these days, the average young person is spending four to five hours a day inside on video games, television and the Internet, and about four minutes a day in what we would say is outdoor, unstructured recreation. We've gone from a generation where your mother had to keep calling you in for dinner, to where parents, albeit dependent on the particular environment or neighborhood they're in, are trying to push their kids more outside, because they seem to be spending all their time on screen time. And we've got to get back to a balance.[70]

Many studies have looked at video game use and concluded that gaming contributes to obesity. In 2008 the University of Buffalo in New York found that parents who reduced the screen time of their children by 17.5 hours a week saw a significant reduction in their children's weight at the end of the two-year study period. "Results showed that watching television and playing computer games can lead to obesity by reducing the amount of time that children are physically active, or by increasing the amount of food they consume as they engaged in these sedentary behaviors,"[71] said Leonard Epstein, a professor of pediatrics who led the study.

Playing Video Games and Staying Fit

In this case the video game industry has responded to the criticisms. Nintendo, the Japanese game and console developer, has introduced the Wii system, which features a number of games designed to get players off their couches and exercising. For example, Wii players can practice their baseball swings or even participate in a virtual game of tennis while standing in front of their TV sets.

The Wii picks up the motions made by the players, projecting them onto the screen. Moreover, players can install games in the system that can lead them through some intense aerobic workouts.

Many of the Wii's workout programs were designed by legendary Nintendo game developer Shigeru Miyamoto, the original designer of *Donkey Kong*. "When you play the Wii, you move your own body," says Miyamoto. "The user gets a much stronger sense of satisfaction than from just sitting down and staring at the screen."[72]

Similar aerobic workouts can be achieved by participating along with the action in the dance game *Dance Dance Revolution*, which requires players to mimic the steps on-screen while dancing on mats that score the accuracy of their movements. Many physical education teachers have set up screens and mats in their gyms so that students can follow the moves of the virtual dancers. At South Middle School in New York City, gym teacher Bill Hines says his seventh-grade students dash into the gym on the days when they know he will be booting up *Dance Dance Revolution*. "I'll tell you one thing," he says. "They don't run in here like that for basketball."[73]

Students in a West Virginia high school health class stomp to the tunes of Dance Dance Revolution, *a dance game that gets young people up and moving. Schools around the country are trying video games like this one to encourage students to exercise.*

Education officials in West Virginia are so impressed with the game that they have incorporated it into the physical education programs in all 765 public schools in the state. Linda M. Carson, a professor of physical education at the University of West Virginia, helped convince state officials to add the game to the state's gym classes. "I was in a mall walking by the arcade and I saw these kids playing *Dance Dance Revolution* and I was just stunned," she says. "There were all these kids dancing and sweating and actually standing in line and paying money to be physically active. And they were drinking water, not soda. It was a physical educator's dream."[74]

Experts are quick to point out, though, that even games like *Dance Dance Revolution* and the programs designed for the Wii system are no substitute for actually getting outdoors and being physically active. They suggest that a game of virtual tennis played on the Wii would probably be most effective if it sparks an interest in real tennis, prompting the player to find a racket and a court and to give the sport a real-life try. Says nutrition expert Lisa Young, "I can't imagine that playing a video game, even the Wii, will burn the same amount of calories compared with going outside and exercising, but it could be a good start for people who never exercise."[75]

Difficult Years Ahead

While games such as *Dance Dance Revolution* and the programs for the Wii do get some players off their couches and exercising, most video game players prefer to play their games while sitting down. Statistics on obesity among young people would seem to support that fact.

Many of these players are also neglecting their schoolwork. Certainly, some schools, like Quest to Learn, have found ways to incorporate video games into their curricula. But popular video games such as *Call of Duty, Left 4 Dead,* and *Gran Turismo* will probably never see the inside of a classroom. As for the video game players who prefer those games and cannot seem to tear themselves away from the action to do their homework or get some exercise, they may be looking forward to some difficult years ahead.

Facts

- A 2007 study published in the journal *Cyber Psychology and Behavior* found that excessive video game play can be linked directly to lower scores on the Scholastic Aptitude Test, which many colleges consider in assessing applicants for admission.

- The journal *Annals of General Psychiatry* reported the results of a 2006 study that found teenagers who suffer from attention deficit hyperactivity disorder (ADHD) and play video games for more than one hour a day exhibit more intense symptoms of the disorder than teenage ADHD patients who play less than an hour a day.

- According to a study reported in the journal *Pediatrics*, players exert about 2.5 times more energy playing Wii bowling and *Dance Dance Revolution* than they do simply watching TV.

- A study by the University of Rochester in New York found that video game play improves driving skills. Researchers concluded that following the action on game screens makes a driver more aware of his or her surroundings, such as spotting a child running into the street to retrieve a ball.

- A study of 872 children in Switzerland linked obesity directly to video game play. The study found that non-Swiss children residing in the country watch more TV and play more video games than native Swiss children and are twice as likely as native Swiss children to be obese.

- Trainers are now relying on video games to give players virtual experiences they would find on their jobs: Firefighters train by playing *HazMat: Hotzone*, financial analysts can play *Forex Trader*, and college administrators can play *Virtual U*. Meanwhile, the U.S. Army distributes the game *America's Army* as a recruiting tool.

CHAPTER FIVE

Should Video Games Be Regulated?

Given all the concerns about video games—that they are addictive and socially isolating, that they encourage real-life violence, and that they get in the way of schoolwork and exercise—politicians have made several efforts to restrict the access of young people to their content. The first attempt to restrict video game content was made in 2000 in St. Louis, Missouri, when county officials adopted an ordinance barring minors from buying video games with violent scenarios. Elsewhere, officials in Indianapolis, Indiana, as well as Oklahoma, Illinois, Louisiana, California, and Washington State have passed similar measures.

Advocacy groups favoring outright censorship or laws restricting sales of games based on their content insist that parents should have some measure of control over the content of the games their children are playing. "It's an issue about giving parents a chance when they go up against an industry,"[76] says Daphne White, executive director of the Lion and Lamb Project, a group that opposes violent content in children's entertainment.

The video game industry has vigorously opposed government controls over the content of the games or restrictions on who may buy the games. Video game developers contend that they enjoy the same First Amendment right to free speech that has been awarded under the U.S. Constitution to film and TV producers as well as book publishers. "This is fundamentally . . . a case about the constitutional status of video games and our belief that regulation of this sort doesn't pass constitutional muster," says Douglas

Lowenstein of the Entertainment Software Association. "The entertainment industries are easy targets. . . . People want to believe the problem of violence in this country is easily solved by making less violent video games and movies."[77]

Lowenstein made those comments shortly before the legality of the St. Louis ordinance was argued in court. Under the law passed by the St. Louis County Council, retailers could be fined if they sold video games that included violent content to minors without their parents' consent. Lowenstein's group challenged the St. Louis law on First Amendment grounds—that the measure violated the game developers' right to free speech. In the St. Louis case, and in all other cases in which government officials have tried to censor game content or restrict the sales of games, the courts have agreed with the Entertainment Software Association's position: Restricting the sales of video games based on their content, or ordering game developers to remove content from the games, is a violation of the First Amendment of the U.S. Constitution.

A History of Censorship

The First Amendment, ratified in 1791 as part of the Bill of Rights, guarantees the right of free speech, meaning the government cannot regulate the content of books, movies, and similar media. Despite efforts by the Founding Fathers to ensure a free and uncensored marketplace of ideas in American society, over the course of American history there have been many attempts to regulate the content of published, cinematic, and electronic media. For the most part these efforts have failed.

In years past, politicians adopted laws banning literature with sexually suggestive themes, denying Americans access to such books *as Lady Chatterley's Lover* by D.H. Lawrence, *Ulysses* by James Joyce, *Lolita* by Vladimir Nabokov, and *Tropic of Cancer* by Henry Miller. In 1961 the American publisher Grove Press tested these laws and published *Tropic of Cancer* in the United States. The book was seized as obscene by government officials in 21 states. Grove Press challenged the seizures, and in 1964 the U.S. Supreme Court threw out all state anti-obscenity laws, finding that they violated the free speech rights of authors and publishers.

"People want to believe the problem of violence in this country is easily solved by making less violent video games and movies."[77]

— Douglas Lowenstein, Entertainment Software Association.

The Family Entertainment and Protection Act

Advocates for restricting sales of violent video games to minors contend that the current parental warning system does not work because it is administered by the video game industry. In other words, the people responsible for labeling the content are the same people who design and produce the content. Critics suggest this is a conflict of interest, because producers of video games are primarily interested in selling the games, and therefore they may misrepresent the levels of violence in the games so that the games may be sold to more customers.

Federal legislators proposed a measure of outside control over the ratings system when they introduced the Family Entertainment Protection Act in 2005. Under the terms of the act, the Federal Trade Commission would be given responsibility for monitoring the ratings system and ensuring that the ratings match the content.

However, the bill also sought to penalize store owners for selling AO- or M-rated games to underage buyers. Similar attempts at restricting sales to minors have been made by state and local governments, and all have been found unconstitutional by the courts. The Family Entertainment Protection Act was never passed by Congress—after the state laws were successfully challenged in the courts, the federal sponsors decided not to bring their bill to the floor for a vote.

Free speech protections would soon be extended to filmmakers. In 1967 U.S. Customs agents seized prints of the Swedish film *I Am Curious (Yellow)* as they arrived in the United States for distribution to theaters. The film told a story about a young Swedish woman's involvement in her country's political controversies (in reality, there really was not that much of a plot to the film—many critics found the story boring). However, the movie contained numerous frank and bold sex scenes, which is what prompted its seizure at the border. The film's distributors challenged the seizure, and in 1969 the courts ruled that the government had no right to deny freedom of speech to the movie's American distributors. Soon after the courts cleared the way for the distribution of the film, the movie's director, Vilgot Sjoman said, "If you have something to say, you're on safe ground."[78]

Virtually the only instances in which the courts have approved the regulation of so-called intellectual content has been in cases involving child pornography. The courts have barred the production, commerce, and ownership of such films and literature, finding child pornography is so contrary to acceptable moral standards that its existence cannot be justified on free speech grounds. The courts have found that despite the violent and sexual material that can be found in many video games, the content of these games falls well short of the line that would equate the games with what can be found in examples of child pornography.

Barring Sales to Minors

Given the very substantial constitutional protections provided under the First Amendment, political leaders have not tried to dictate to video game developers what type of content they can program into the games. In other words, government regulators do not want to go into the business of dictating plots or dialogue or telling artists how to draw the human figure. Instead, they have sought to police sales of the games to minors. In 2005 California governor Arnold Schwarzenegger signed a law banning sales or rentals of video games with violent content to minors. Schwarzenegger declared:

> Today I signed legislation to ensure parent involvement in determining which video games are appropriate for their children. The bill I signed will require violent video games be clearly labeled and not sold to children under 18 years old. Many of these games are made for adults, and choosing games that are appropriate for kids should be a decision made by their parents.[79]

Many critics of the law found a large measure of irony in Schwarzenegger's support for the measure. Prior to his election as governor, Schwarzenegger forged a very successful career as a Hollywood actor, mostly starring in action-packed films containing an abundance of violent content, including the 1984 hit *The Terminator*. In 1990 the first of several video game versions of *The Terminator* was produced. "It's kind of ironic he's protecting kids from himself,"[80] insisted Jason Della Rocca, executive director of the International Game Developers Association, which opposed the law.

The California law was tossed out by a court in 2007 on the grounds that it violated the free speech rights of the game developers. Essentially, the court ruled, barring the sales of a video game to a segment of the population restrains the right of the game developer to express ideas to those people, regardless of their ages. Similar rulings were rendered in the other cases. In the St. Louis case, for example, the U.S. Court of Appeals took note that in even the most violent video games, the games do tell stories and provide artistic content. "[Video games] are as much entitled to the protection of free speech as the best of literature,"[81] the court's opinion said.

Failed Efforts to Regulate Sales

Despite these setbacks, political leaders keep trying. Before he left office in a bribery scandal, Illinois governor Rod Blagojevich proposed a law that would ban sales to minors of video games displaying realistic depictions of "human on human violence."[82] Blagojevich proposed the law after a foreign video game developer started marketing a game titled *JFK Reloaded*, in which players can reenact the 1963 assassination of President John F. Kennedy. Blagojevich said he found the game so repugnant that he was sure the courts would agree, finding it contrary to acceptable moral standards. Said Blagojevich, "Just as a child buying cigarettes is inappropriate, just as a child buying alcohol is inappropriate, just as a child buying pornography is inappropriate, the same kind of thinking, in my judgment, applies to violent video games and graphic sexual video games."[83]

"Many of these games are made for adults, and choosing games that are appropriate for kids should be a decision made by their parents."[79]

— California governor Arnold Schwarzenegger.

Legal experts did not find themselves in agreement with the governor. Said Geoffrey Stone, a University of Chicago law professor, "[The Blagojevich law] is hopeless because there is no recognized constitutional principle that allows the government to shield children from violent expression."[84] Blagojevich pushed ahead, though, and in 2005 the Illinois General Assembly adopted the law. Members of the video game industry soon filed a court challenge, and by the end of the year a federal court had declared the Illinois law unconstitutional.

Still, local political leaders continue to press for laws that would regulate the sales of violent video games to children. In 2009 Schwarzenegger appealed the California decision to the U.S. Supreme Court. Meanwhile, several bills are currently in the U.S. House and U.S. Senate; those bills all seek some degree of censorship or regulation over video game content. Experts say that there is little chance that any of these bills will end up on the president's desk anytime soon.

While governor of Illinois, Rod Blagojevich urged Chicago transit officials to cancel contracts for violent video game ads on city buses such as this one. Blagojevich convinced state lawmakers to ban sales to minors of games with realistic violence, but that law was later deemed unconstitutional.

A Code of Ethics

Although the video game industry has consistently opposed efforts by lawmakers to restrict sales, industry officials are receptive to the notion that constant scenes of violent or sexually explicit content are not suitable for young viewers. In fact, during the early years of the industry, some video game companies took the

What Are Internet Flash Games?

Some of the most offensive and violent video games are not produced by professional game developers but by amateurs who make them available for free on the Internet. These games are known as Internet flash games. Among them are *Border Patrol*, in which players shoot illegal immigrants as they attempt to cross the border into the United States, and *V-Tech Rampage*, in which players can reenact the 2007 campus shootings at Virginia Tech University.

Lawmakers who call for legislation controlling sales of violent video games often cite the availability of these titles as reasons the laws are necessary. "It is imperative that we find a way to prevent these virtual realities from continuing to fuel and teach violent behavior which is corrupting our youth," insisted Andrew Lanza, a New York state senator.

Industry insiders quickly point out, though, that policing the availability of these games through legislation is impossible. They argue that there is no way to stop an amateur from designing a game and making it widely available on the Internet. "Sometimes, I think [legislators] genuinely don't understand the difference between commercial and noncommercial games," says Dennis McCauley, editor of the Game Politics Web site. "But sometimes they bring it up just to add a little hype and shock value to their argument."

Quoted in Lara Crigger, "Your Tax Dollars at Work," *Games for Windows*, March 2008.

position that violent or sexually explicit content would not be a part of their business.

As far back as the early 1980s, Atari declared it would not permit graphic depictions of violence in its games. Said Nolan Bushnell: "We were really unhappy with [*Death Race*]. We had an internal rule that we wouldn't allow violence against people. You could blow up a tank or you could blow up a flying saucer, but you couldn't blow up people. We felt that was not good form, and we adhered to that all during my tenure."[85]

Nintendo also took that position. The company adopted a code of ethics dictating that games sold for the company's systems could not include profanity or depict nudity, violence, or graphic illustrations of death. This was the company that had introduced the lovable character Mario in the *Donkey Kong* series and was also producing games for very young players based on the Pokémon characters. Nintendo appeared to be carving itself out a strict niche of family-friendly entertainment. Indeed, when *Mortal Kombat* entered the market in 1993, Nintendo insisted that the game's developer produce a sanitized version for the company's consoles.

Parent advocacy groups applauded Nintendo's position, but when the company's competitors made the uncensored version of *Mortal Kombat* available for their game systems, Nintendo found that its code of ethics was costing it valuable profits. Eventually, the company decided to drop its code of ethics. "We got a lot of plaudits for [the code of ethics] in public—and got killed in the sales arena," says George Harrison, vice president of marketing for Nintendo of America. "We just felt to compete in the hardware area we had to increase our share of that older audience."[86]

"Just as a child buying cigarettes is inappropriate, just as a child buying alcohol is inappropriate, just as a child buying pornography is inappropriate, the same kind of thinking, in my judgment, applies to violent video games and graphic sexual video games."[83]

— Former Illinois governor Rod Blagojevich.

Rating the Games

Such efforts by the companies themselves to restrict game content may have failed, but the industry has still taken steps to help ensure that young viewers are not exposed to mature game content. In 1994 the industry established a voluntary ratings system to guide parents, alerting them to the content of the games.

The system is similar to the rating system adopted by the movie industry in the 1960s. Although movie producers and theater owners felt they were on firm legal ground, they still acknowledged that the content of many films was not suitable for young viewers. And so the Motion Picture Association of America and the National Association of Theater Owners established a rating system. Under the system, members of a panel sponsored by the two organizations, the Classification and Rating Administration, view films and rate them according to their content. These ratings—G, PG, PG-13, R, and NC-17—guide theater owners, who will, for example, bar viewers under the age of 17 from admission into an NC-17 rated film. Enforcement of the ratings is voluntary—no theater owner breaks the law by letting an underage person buy a ticket to an NC-17 rated film. Nevertheless, most theater owners are believed to maintain a strict adherence to the ratings system. (In 1985 the recording industry also adopted a voluntary parental warning policy, placing stickers on compact disks containing music with explicit lyrics. Also, in 1997 TV producers adopted voluntary parental warnings for broadcast content.)

Following the lead of the movie industry, the Entertainment Software Association established a similar review panel, the Entertainment Software Rating Board (ESRB), to provide ratings for video games. The ratings are marked clearly on the game packaging, visible to merchants and customers. The ratings include:

EC: Early Childhood; the game contains no material that parents would find objectionable, and all content is suitable for children age three and older.

E: Everyone; the content could include minimal cartoon violence, fantasy, mild violence, and infrequent use of mild language. Overall, the content is suitable for children age six and older.

E-10+: Everyone age 10 and older; in these games, the content may contain a somewhat higher level of violence and stronger language than what is found in E, but the violent content is still relatively mild.

T: Teen; game content is suitable for ages 13 and older. The content could include violence, suggestive themes, crude humor, minimal depictions of blood, simulated gambling, and infrequent use of strong language.

M: Mature; titles rated M are suitable for players 17 and older. The games in this category may include intense violence as well as graphic depictions of blood, gore, and sexual content. Strong language and the frequent use of profanities are often featured in games rated M.

AO: Adults Only; in games rated AO, the content is suitable for adults age 18 and older. The content of AO games may include prolonged and graphic scenes of intense violence, gore, nudity, and sexual content.

RP: Rating Pending; these games have been submitted to the ESRB but a ruling has not been made. The RP rating does not appear on the box that is sold to the public, but only in the advertisements for the game prior to its release and its final board rating.

In addition, on the back of the game box the developer lists more specific information about the game's content, stating which elements of the game prompted the ESRB to select its rating. Typical descriptions found on the backs of the boxes may include comic mischief, blood and gore, intense violence, partial nudity, strong sexual content, strong language, and use of drugs.

Underage Buyers

As with the film ratings, enforcement of the video game ratings by merchants is voluntary. Many critics do not believe merchants do a very good job of enforcing the ratings, arguing that many merchants are simply interested in selling the games and turning a profit and do not pay much attention to the age of customers who buy the games. In fact, a 2003 study by the Federal Trade Commission found that retailers do a poor job of enforcing the ratings system—the study found that 69 percent of buyers between the ages of 13 and 16 are able to buy games rated M for mature, even though that rating should be alerting the merchants

10 Most Frequently Played Games and Their Ratings

In 2008 teenagers were playing many different types of video games. The range of games indicated that they were not always playing violent, or M-rated, games. Fifty percent of the games played were rated E, meaning that the content was suitable for anyone six years old and up.

10 Most Frequently Played Games

Game Title	ESRB Rating
Guitar Hero	Teen
Halo 3	Mature
Madden NFL (no specific version)	Everyone
Solitaire	Everyone
Dance Dance Revolution	Everyone
Madden NFL 08	Everyone
Tetris	Everyone
Grand Theft Auto (no specific version)	Mature
Halo (no specific version)	Mature
The Sims (no specific version)	Teen

Sources: Pew Internet & American Life Project, "Teens, Video Games and Civics," September 2008. www.pewinternet.org; Entertainment Software Rating Board, "ESRB Game Ratings." www.esrb.org.

that the content of the games is not suitable for players under the age of 17. A similar study commissioned for the New York City Council found that 16-year-old customers were able to buy M-rated video games on 90 percent of their attempts.

Those statistics do not come as a surprise to the National Institute on Media and the Family, which has occasionally run its own tests—sending 9- and 10-year-old children into stores to see if merchants will sell them M-rated games. David Walsh, president of the organization, says he is never shocked when a young child comes out of a store with a copy of *Grand Theft Auto: San Andreas* in hand. He says:

> With the retailers, it's a mixed bag. Parents think that retailers should have a policy similar to the theater policy, which is that you don't sell an M-rated game to a minor without parental permission. The problem is that, although most of the major chains have that policy in place, they don't enforce it. And so we've had a 9-year-old go into a number of stores . . . and have no trouble buying that game whatsoever.[87]

And critics also point out that video games are often promoted by celebrities, whose endorsements help sell the games to their fans. Hip-hop star 50 Cent, for example, has urged his fans to buy a game in which he is featured as the main character. The game, *True Crime: New York City*, is regarded as one of the most violent video games on the market. And yet 50 Cent has said, "Just because it is rated mature doesn't mean you shouldn't buy it for your kids."[88] Given that type of influence on young buyers, critics suggest, it should not come as a surprise to learn that many young gamers can find ways to obtain the games they want to play.

Are the Ratings Effective?

Moreover, there are differing opinions on whether the ratings are effective. One survey sponsored by the video game industry reported that 83 percent of parents say they pay close attention to the ratings of the games their children play. In addition, the survey found, 74 percent of parents say they check the ratings in the stores before letting their children buy the games.

Says Patricia Vance, president of the ESRB:

> Virtually every computer and video game sold in the U.S. today carries an ESRB rating and nearly all major retailers choose to only stock games that have been rated by our

"Just because it is rated mature doesn't mean you shouldn't buy it for your kids."[88]

— Hip-hop star 50 Cent.

organization. This voluntary commitment from the video game industry and the retail community ensures that consumers have accurate and reliable information to help them decide which games are appropriate for themselves, their children and other family members. Today, the vast majority of parents use and trust ESRB ratings in helping them make those decisions.[89]

Critics are not so sure. Walsh says he finds many parents maintain an aloof attitude about the content of the games and do not pay much attention to the ratings on the boxes. "Our experience shows that unless parents themselves are gamers, they tend to be pretty uninformed," he says. "Parents don't realize that the goal of [*Grand Theft Auto: Vice City*] is to become a more proficient sociopath."[90]

Controversies Will Continue

In the years since Steve Russell developed *Spacewar!* and the first *Pong* games were installed in bars and bowling alleys, the development of video games has grown into an industry worth tens of billions of dollars. And there is no question that the growth of the industry is due largely to demand for games that contain mature content. For years games rated M have represented the fastest growing segment of the video game market.

Along with that growth has come controversy. Players like Shawn Woolley become so addicted and socially isolated in their play that they do not realize the games have taken over their lives. Meanwhile, in Virginia, a little boy figured out how to drive his parents' car by playing *Grand Theft Auto*, while in Tennessee two other boys failed to understand the difference between shooting at virtual cars on their TV screen and shooting at real cars speeding down the nearby interstate highway. In addition, a debate rages over whether video games are responsible for declining test scores and bulging waistlines.

These issues are not likely to be resolved soon. Government leaders have attempted to address some of these matters by calling for restrictions on sales of violent games to minors, but their efforts often run counter to the constitutional principles on which

America was founded. Therefore, it is likely that players of all ages will continue playing all manner of games—even those that may not be suitable for them—while game developers will continue to find ways to astound their senses.

Facts

- A 2008 study by the Federal Trade Commission found that retailers enforce the voluntary video game rating code by refusing to sell M-rated games to under-17 customers just 80 percent of the time.

- The Entertainment Software Association reports that 84 percent of games sold in America are rated either E, E-10+, or T.

- In 2007 legislators in New York State proposed a law that mandated a minimum of one year in prison for merchants who are convicted of selling violent video games to underage buyers.

- A poll commissioned by Hill & Knowlton, a New York public relations firm, found that 60 percent of Americans favor government regulation of video game sales.

- According to the Entertainment Software Rating Board, about 10 percent of video games on the market are rated M.

- In Oklahoma a 2006 bill to restrict the sales of violent video games to minors was adopted by the State House of Representatives by a vote of 98-0 and the State Senate by a vote of 47-0; a year later a judge ruled the law unconstitutional.

Related Organizations

American Civil Liberties Union (ACLU)

125 Broad St., 18th Floor
New York, NY 10004
phone: (212) 549-2500
e-mail: aclu@aclu.org
Web site: www.aclu.org

The ACLU has spent many years opposing government efforts to censor books, movies, and other forms of media. By following the link for "Key Issues" on the organization's Web site, visitors can read the status of many First Amendment rights cases in which the ACLU is involved.

Center for Media and Public Affairs (CMPA)

2100 L St. NW, Suite 300
Washington, DC 20037
phone: (202) 223-2942
fax: (202) 872-4014
e-mail: mail@cmpa.com
Web site: www.cmpa.com

The CMPA conducts research on how the media affect Americans. By following the link to Entertainment Studies, visitors to the CMPA Web page can download copies of the reports *TV Goes PG but Movies Are Still R Rated: Changes in Sex and Violence in Popular Culture* and *Merchandizing Mayhem: Violence in Popular Entertainment*.

Children Now

1212 Broadway, 5th Floor
Oakland, CA 94612

phone: (510) 763-2444
fax: (510) 763-1974
e-mail: info@childrennow.org
Web site: www.childrennow.org

Children Now is a national advocacy group that studies trends and issues affecting children, including the availability of junk food and content of TV and radio programs. Visitors to the organization's Web site can download a copy of the report *Fair Play? Violence, Gender and Race in Video Games.*

Entertainment Software Association (ESA)

575 Seventh St. NW, Suite 300
Washington, DC 20004
e-mail: esa@theesa.com
Web site: www.theesa.com

The ESA is the trade association representing the companies that publish and market video games. On the Web site's public policy link, students can read updates of the legal fights the organization has waged against efforts to censor games or restrict their sales to minors. Transcripts of testimony by ESA officials defending the industry's efforts to self-regulate are also available.

Entertainment Software Rating Board (ESRB)

317 Madison Ave., 22nd Floor
New York, NY 10017
phone: (212) 759-0700
e-mail: info@esrb.org
Web site: www.esrb.org

Established by the Entertainment Software Association, the board provides ratings so that consumers can understand the content of the games before they buy them. Visitors to the ESRB Web site can find definitions of each rating and the criteria the board uses to rate the games, as well as information and ratings on specific games.

Federal Trade Commission (FTC)

600 Pennsylvania Ave. NW
Washington, DC 20580

phone: (202) 326-2222
Web site: www.ftc.gov

The FTC monitors video game use and has issued reports on the industry, including *Video Games: Reading the Ratings on the Games People Play*, which students can find on the agency's Web page. Students can also find transcripts of testimony by FTC officials who have commented on the effects of violent video game play on young people.

Free Expression Policy Project (FEPP)

170 W. Seventy-sixth St., No. 301
New York, NY 10023
Web site: www.fepproject.org

The FEPP tracks efforts by governments to censor the media and also provides legal assistance to individuals and organizations fighting for free speech rights. In Indianapolis, Indiana, the FEPP filed a brief opposing an ordinance regulating video game sales. That brief can be accessed on the organization's Web site along with commentaries on many free speech issues.

International Game Developers Association (IGDA)

19 Mantua Rd.
Mt. Royal, NJ 08061
phone: (856) 423-2990
fax: (856) 423-3420
e-mail: contact@igda.org
Web site: www.igda.org

The trade association represents professionals who design and produce video games. Visitors to the IGDA Web site can find resources on the organization's anticensorship campaigns by following the link to "Advocacy." Also available are essays and columns on censorship written by IGDA officials, as well as legal briefs filed by attorneys in censorship cases.

Kaiser Family Foundation

2400 Sand Hill Rd.
Menlo Park, CA 94025

phone: (650) 854-9400
fax: (650) 854-4800
Web site: www.kff.org

The foundation studies issues that affect the health of Americans and has examined many topics involving the impact of media on young people. Visitors to the foundation's Web site can download copies of the reports *Key Facts: Children and Video Games* and *Media Multi-tasking: Changing the Amount and Nature of Young People's Media Use*.

National Institute on Media and the Family

606 Twenty-fourth Ave. S., Suite 606
Minneapolis, MN 55454
phone: (888) 672-5437
fax: (612) 672-4113
e-mail: info@drdavidwalsh.com
Web site: www.mediafamily.org

The institute has initiated many projects designed to rein in the violence and strong sexual content found in video games. By following the link to "Hot Topics," students can find many resources and reports by the institute on video game and Internet addiction.

Pew Internet & American Life Project

1615 L St. NW, Suite 700
Washington, DC 20036
phone: (202) 415-4500
fax: (202) 419-4505
e-mail: data@pewinternet.org
Web site: www.pewinternet.org

A division of the Pew Research Center, a nonprofit group that examines public policy issues in America, the Pew Internet & American Life Project focuses on the impact of digital media on Americans. Visitors to the organization's Web site can download the Pew report *Teens, Video Games and Civics*, which examines whether young video game players are involved in their communities.

Wayne County Prosecutor Kym L. Worthy

Frank Murphy Hall of Justice
1441 St. Antoine St.
Detroit, MI 48226
phone: (313) 224-5777
fax: (313) 224-0974
Web site: www.waynecounty.com/mygovt/prosecutor

Each year, Wayne County prosecutor Kym L. Worthy releases a list of the video games she finds containing the most violent content. Visitors to the prosecutor's Web site can find information on each year's list by following the link to "Press Releases."

For Further Research

Books

Craig A. Anderson, Douglas A. Gentile, Katherine E. Buckley, *Violent Video Game Effects on Children and Adolescents: Theory, Research and Public Policy*. Oxford, England: Oxford University Press, 2007.

Simon Egenfeldt-Nielson, Jonas Heide Smith and Susana Pajares Tosca, *Understanding Video Games: The Essential Introduction*. New York: Routledge, 2008.

David M. Haugen and Susan Musser, eds., *Media Violence*. Farmington Hills, MI: Greenhaven, 2009.

Steven J. Kirsh, *Media and Youth: A Developmental Perspective*. Oxford, England: Wiley-Blackwell, 2009.

Lawrence Kutner and Cheryl K. Olson, *Grand Theft Childhood: The Surprising Truth About Violent Video Games*. New York: Simon & Schuster, 2008.

Bill Loguidice and Matt Barton, *Vintage Games: An Insider Look at the History of Grand Theft Auto, Super Mario, and the Most Influential Games of All Time*. Burlington, MA: Focal Press, 2009.

Periodicals

Lara Crigger, "Your Tax Dollars at Work," *Games for Windows*, March 2008.

Andrew Klein, "Gamers Get Moving," *Scholastic Super Science*, March 2009.

David Kusher, "Can Video Games Teach Kids?" *Parade*, December 20, 2009.

Laurel J. Sweet and Marie Szanislo, "The 911 on Video Game Obsession," *Boston Herald*, December 21, 2009.

Tad Walch, "Student Researches Effects of Video Games," *Deseret News*, January 23, 2009.

David Zizzo, "Realities of Virtual Obsession," *Daily Oklahoman*, September 2, 2008.

Web Sites

Addictions (www.apa.org/topics/addiction/index.aspx). Maintained by the American Psychological Association, the Web page provides definitions and background information on addictions. Visitors can learn how to recognize addictions and read many news stories about different types of addictive behaviors.

Gamer Widow (http://gamerwidow.com). The Internet site established by Sherry Myrow helps family members develop strategies for weaning loved ones away from video games. Visitors can find advice, blog entries, and news stories about video game addiction.

When Two Tribes Go to War: A History of the Video Game Controversy (www.gamespot.com/features/6090892). Maintained by the online game review site GameSpot, the page provides an in-depth history of video game violence and efforts by government officials to regulate the industry.

Source Notes

Introduction: When Video Games Are More than Just Games

1. Quoted in Tom Jackman, "Boy, 6, Misses Bus, Takes Mom's Car Instead," *Washington Post*, January 7, 2009. www.washington post.com.

2. Ryan MacDonald, "*Grand Theft Auto* Review," GameSpot, May 6, 1998. www.gamespot.com.

3. Tom Orry, "*killer7* Review," Videogamer, July 17, 2005. www. videogamer.com.

4. David Walsh, "Watching Video Games for 10 Years," National Institute on Media and the Family, 2009. www.mediafamily. org.

Chapter One: What Are the Origins of Today's Video Game Controversies?

5. Quoted in Steven Kent, *The Ultimate History of Video Games*. New York: Three Rivers, 2001, p. 44.

6. Quoted in Benjamin H. Alexander, "Impact of Computers on Human Behavior," *Vital Speeches of the Day*, January 1, 1983, p. 186.

7. Quoted in Associated Press, "Over Half of U.S. Adults Play Computer Games," CBC News, December 8, 2008. www. cbc.ca.

8. Quoted in Arthur Asa Berger, *Video Games: A Popular Cultural Phenomenon*. New Brunswick, NJ: Transaction, 2002, p. 81.

9. Quoted in Mark J.P. Wolf, ed., *The Medium of the Video Game*. Austin: University of Texas Press, 2001, p. 40.

10. Quoted in Kent, *The Ultimate History of Video Games*, p. 227.

11. Quoted in Lawrence Kutner and Cheryl K. Olson, *Grand Theft Childhood: The Surprising Truth About Violent Video Games.* New York: Simon & Schuster, 2008, p. 60.

12. N'Gai Croal and Jane Hughes, "Lara Croft, the Bit Girl," *Newsweek*, November 10, 1997, p. 82.

13. Children Now, *Fair Play? Violence, Race and Gender in Video Games*, December 1, 2001. www.childrennow.org.

14. Children Now, *Fair Play? Violence, Race and Gender in Video Games*.

15. David Walsh, Douglas Gentile, and Marilyn VanOverbeke, *MediaWise Video Game Report Card*, National Institute on Media and the Family, December 19, 2002. www.mediafamily. org.

16. Leigh Alexander, "And You Thought *Grand Theft Auto* Was Bad: Should the United States Ban a Japanese 'Rape Simulator' Game?" *Slate*, March 9, 2009. www.slate.com.

Chapter Two: Do Violent Video Games Promote Real-Life Violence?

17. Quoted in David Kushner, "Grand Death Auto," *Salon*, February 22, 2005. http://dir.salon.com.

18. Quoted in Gregory K. Moffatt, *Blind-Sided: Homicide When It Is Least Expected.* Westport, CT: Praeger, 2000, p. 143.

19. Moffatt, *Blind-Sided*, p. 144.

20. Quoted in Jim Herron Zamora, "'Nut Case' Trial Set to Begin," *San Francisco Chronicle*, February 6, 2006, p. A-1.

21. Quoted in Alex Tresniowski, Siobhan Morrissey, John Anderson, Nancy Wistach, and Lori Rozsa, "Driven to Kill?" *People*, September 26, 2005, p. 97.

22. Quoted in Cynthia Carter and C. Kay Weaver, *Violence and the Media*. Philadelphia: Open University Press, 2003, p. 42.

23. American Psychological Association, "Childhood Exposure to Media Violence Predicts Young Adult Aggressive Behavior, According to a New 15-Year Study," press release, March 9, 2003. www.apa.org.

24. American Psychological Association, "Childhood Exposure to Media Violence Predicts Young Adult Aggressive Behavior, According to a New 15-Year Study."

25. Jonathan L. Freedman, *Media Violence and Its Effect on Aggression: Assessing the Scientific Evidence.* Toronto, ON: University of Toronto Press, 2002, p. 176.

26. National Youth Violence Prevention Resource Center, "Prevalence of Media Violence," February 26, 2008. www.safeyouth.org.

27. Quoted in CBS News, "Can a Video Game Lead to Murder?" March 4, 2005. www.cbsnews.com.

28. Quoted in Dirk Johnson and James Brooke, "Portrait of Outcasts Seeking to Stand Out from Other Groups," *New York Times*, April 22, 1999, p. 1.

29. Quoted in Kushner, "Grand Death Auto."

30. Quoted in Kushner, "Grand Death Auto."

31. Quoted in Kristin Kalning, "Does Game Violence Make Teens Aggressive?" MSNBC, December 8, 2006. www.msnbc.msn.com.

32. Henry Jenkins, "Reality Bytes: Eight Myths About Video Games Debunked," PBS, 2004. www.pbs.org.

33. Jenkins, "Reality Bytes."

34. Quoted in Tresniowski, Morrissey, Anderson, Wistach, and Rozsa, "Driven to Kill?" p. 97.

Chapter Three: Do Video Games Lead to Addiction and Social Isolation?

35. Quoted in *48 Hours*, "Addicted: Suicide over *EverQuest*?" CBS News, October 18, 2002. www.cbsnews.com.

36. Quoted in David Zizzo, "Realities of Virtual Obsession," *Daily Oklahoman*, September 2, 2008. http://newsok.com.

37. Quoted in Zizzo, "Realities of Virtual Obsession."

38. Quoted in Michael D. Lemonick, "How We Get Addicted," *Time*, July 5, 2007. www.time.com.

39. Quoted in *Talk of the Nation*, "Compulsive Video Gaming: Addiction or Vice?" National Public Radio, July 10, 2007. www.npr.org.

40. Quoted in *Talk of the Nation*, "Compulsive Video Gaming."

41. Quoted in Laurel J. Sweet and Marie Szanislo, "The 911 on Video Game Obsession," *Boston Herald*, December 21, 2009. www.bostonherald.com.

42. Quoted in John DiConsiglio, "Game Over," *Choices*, January 2008, p. 8.

43. Quoted in DiConsiglio, "Game Over," pp. 8–9.

44. Quoted in DiConsiglio, "Game Over," p. 9.

45. Quoted in Science Daily, "Video Games Linked to Poor Relationships with Friends, Family," January 25, 2009. www.sciencedaily.com.

46. Quoted in Science Daily, "Video Games Linked to Poor Relationships with Friends, Family."

47. Quoted in Tad Walch, "Student Researches Effects of Video Games," *Deseret News*, January 23, 2009. www.deseretnews.com.

48. Quoted in BBC News, "South Korean Dies After Games Session," August 10, 2005. http://news.bbc.co.uk.

49. Quoted in *Times* (London), "Boy Collapses After Playing *World of Warcraft* for 24 Hours Straight," November 17, 2008. http://technology.timesonline.co.uk.

50. Quoted in *Times* (London), "Boy Collapses After Playing *World of Warcraft* for 24 Hours Straight."

51. Quoted in BBC News, "South Korean Dies After Games Session."

52. Amanda Lenhart, Joseph Kahne, Ellen Middaugh, Alexandra Rankin Macgill, Chris Evans, and Jessica Vitak, *Teens, Video Games and Civics*. Washington, DC: Pew Internet & American Life Project, 2008, p. iii. http://pewinternet.org.

53. Lenhart, Kahne, Middaugh, Macgill, Evans, and Vitak, *Teens, Video Games and Civics*, p. 42.

54. Richard T.A. Wood, "Problems with the Concept of Video Game 'Addiction': Some Case Study Examples," *International Journal of Mental Health and Addiction*, June 2008, p. 169.

55. Rob Cover, "Gaming Addiction: Discourse, Identity, Time and Play in the Production of the Gamer Addiction Myth," *Game Studies*, December 2006. http://gamestudies.org.

56. Cover, "Gaming Addiction."

57. Quoted in *48 Hours*, "Addicted."

58. Quoted in DiConsiglio, "Game Over," p. 9.

Chapter Four: Do Young Gamers Risk Their Health and Well-Being?

59. Quoted in Katherine Nguyen, "Video Game Addiction All Too Real," *Orange County (CA) Register*, January 28, 2007. www.ocregister.com.

60. Quoted in Karen Goldberg Goff, "Screened Out," *Washington Times*, April 10, 2005, p. D-1.

61. Marny R. Hauge and Douglas A. Gentile, *Video Game Addiction Among Adolescents: Associations with Academic Performance and Aggression*, paper presented at the Society for Research in Child Development Conference, Tampa, Florida, April 2003. www.psychology.iastate.edu.

62. Quoted in *Tell Me More*, "Study: Kids Fixated with Television, Internet and Texting," National Public Radio, January 26, 2010.

63. Quoted in Goff, "Screened Out," p. D-1.

64. Quoted in Fred Guterl, Michael Hastings, Jonathan Adams, Mark Russell, Peter Hudson, and Benjamin Sutherland, "Overloaded?" *Newsweek*, September 8, 2003, p. E-4.

65. Quoted in Goff, "Screened Out," p. D-1.

66. Quoted in David Kusher, "Can Video Games Teach Kids?" *Parade*, December 20, 2009, p. 12.

67. Quoted in Kusher, "Can Video Games Teach Kids?" p. 12.

68. Quoted in Kusher, "Can Video Games Teach Kids?" p. 12.

69. Quoted in Matthew Yi, "Playing Games in School: Using Videos Helps Students Love to Learn Their Lessons," *San Francisco Chronicle*, February 20, 2006, p. E-1.

70. Quoted in the transcript of U.S. House Committee on Energy and Commerce, Subcommittee on Health, hearing on childhood obesity, *Political Transcripts*, December 16, 2009.

71. Quoted in Science Daily, "Restricting Kids' Video Time Reduces Obesity, Randomized Trial Shows," March 4, 2008. www.sciencedaily.com.

72. Quoted in Andrew Klein, "Gamers Get Moving," *Scholastic Super Science*, March 2009, p. 12.

73. Quoted in Seth Schiesel, "P.E. Classes Turn to Video Game That Works Legs, Not Thumbs," *New York Times*, April 30, 2007, p. A-1.

74. Quoted in Schiesel, "P.E. Classes Turn to Video Game That Works Legs, Not Thumbs," p. A-1.

75. Quoted in Klein, "Gamers Get Moving," p. 12.

Chapter Five: Should Video Games Be Regulated?

76. Quoted in Mark Jurkowitz, "Appeals Court Holds Key in Battle over Regulation of Violent Video Games," *Boston Globe*, October 2, 2002, p. D-1.

77. Quoted in Jurkowitz, "Appeals Court Holds Key in Battle over Regulation of Violent Video Games," p. D-1.

78. Quoted in Caren Weiner, "*Curious* Under Fire," *Entertainment Weekly*, March 6, 1998, p. 92.

79. Quoted in Dean Takahashi, "Governor Signs Bill on Violent Video Games," *San Jose Mercury News*, October 8, 2005.

80. Quoted in Takahashi, "Governor Signs Bill on Violent Video Games."

81. Quoted in Free Expression Project, "Appeals Court Strikes Down St. Louis Video Games Law," June 3, 2003. www.fepproject.org.

82. Quoted in Anita Hamilton, Anna Macias Aguayo, Noah Isackson, David E. Thigpen, and Laura A. Locke, "Video Vigilantes," *Time*, January 10, 2005, p. 60.

83. Quoted in Hamilton, Aguayo, Isackson, Thigpen, and Locke, "Video Vigilantes," p. 60.

84. Quoted in Hamilton, Aguayo, Isackson, Thigpen, and Locke, "Video Vigilantes," p. 60.

85. Quoted in Kent, *The Ultimate History of Video Games*, p. 92.

86. Quoted in Don Steinberg, "Adult Games Scoring Big with Children," *Philadelphia Inquirer*, December 1, 2002, p. A-1.

87. Quoted in Tavis Smiley, "Kevin Baird and Dave Walsh Discuss Violence in Video Games," National Public Radio, November 18, 2002.

88. Quoted in ABC News, "Is the Video Game Rating System Effective?" November 29, 2005. http://abcnews.go.com.

89. Patricia Vance, transcript of testimony before the U.S. Senate Judiciary Committee, Subcommittee on the Constitution, Civil Rights and Property Rights, *Political Transcripts*, March 29, 2006.

90. Quoted in Steinberg, "Adult Games Scoring Big with Children," p. A-1.

Index

About the Author

Hal Marcovitz, a former newspaper reporter, has written more than 150 books for young readers. His other titles in the In Controversy series include *Is Stem Cell Research Necessary?* and *Can Renewable Energy Replace Fossil Fuels?*